Walking in Virtue

Moral Decisions and Spiritual Growth in Daily Life

John W. Crossin, O.S.F.S.

Paulist Press ◆ New York ◆ Mahwah, N.J.

Library of Congress Cataloging-in-Publication Data

Crossin, John W.
  Walking in virtue : moral decisions and spiritual growth in daily life / John W. Crossin.
    p. cm.
  Includes bibliographical references and index.
  ISBN 0–8091–3834–4 (alk. paper)
  1. Spiritual life—Catholic Church. 2. Christian ethics—Catholic authors. I. Title.
BX2350.2.C77   1998
241'.042—dc21   98–38275
                                                                             CIP

Published by Paulist Press
997 Macarthur Boulevard
Mahwah, New Jersey 07430

www.paulistpress.com

Printed and bound in the
United States of America

Contents

Contents

Acknowledgments

I wish to thank my friends in the De Sales Group, Kevin Barry, Sheila Garcia, Betty Le Buffe and Rowena Muller Morris, for their thoughtful suggestions about this book and its predecessor, *Friendship: The Key to Spiritual Growth.* I am very much indebted to them for their insights and their support in the process of writing. In particular, I wish to thank Sheila Garcia for her work on chapter 1 and Kevin Barry for his contribution to chapter 7.

I wish to acknowledge that some of the materials on the Holy Spirit in chapter 1 and on Humility in chapter 8 originally appeared in the Faith Alive series of the Catholic News Service. I am grateful to the editors of the News Service for their encouragement in using this material. Likewise, I am grateful to Lawrence Boadt, C.S.P. for his wise editorial assistance with this volume.

This book originated in 1995 during a summer sabbatical from my duties as president of De Sales School of Theology. I wish to thank Very Rev. Richard Reece, O.S.F.S., Provincial Superior of the Oblates of St. Francis de Sales at that time, for his encouragement of this project.

Recently, De Sales School of Theology closed its doors after forty-seven years of operation. I wish to dedicate this book to the trustees, faculty, administrators, students, staff, colleagues and friends who made De Sales such a wonderful place to live, learn and grow spiritually.

I am happy to dedicate this book
to the trustees, faculty, administrators,
alumni, students, staff, colleagues and friends of

De Sales School of Theology (1949–97)

Introduction

*T*oday there is widespread interest in "things spiritual." Self-help and "spiritual" volumes fill the bookstores. Even talk-radio "call-ins" touch on matters such as moral decision making and personal integrity. The quest for spiritual and moral wholeness seems widespread.

Many Americans are seeking greater spiritual depth. They are searching for deeper meaning and for ethical clarity in a time of change and transition. This small book addresses those looking for a more profound formation of personal character in the Christian tradition. It discusses Scripture, community and conscience as they both inform and form us. It argues that our daily moral discernments, our moral choices, shape our lives.

In a companion volume published in July of 1997, *Friendship: The Key to Spiritual Growth,* I contended that friendship with self, with others and with God is central to spiritual and moral progress. Good friendships are essential for spiritual growth. Our friends challenge us to learn more, to use our talents and to serve others generously. It is in good relationships that we begin to develop the virtues essential for human happiness. It is in good relationships that we become holy.

In this book, we take a further step and explore some elements which contribute to the development of Christian virtue. The guidance of the Holy Spirit, the study of Scripture, interactions in community, respect for our own and others' human dignity, the formation of conscience and wise moral judgment all help us toward a growing depth

1

and spiritual maturity. We will discuss all of these topics in separate chapters as we proceed.

I hope that our discussions will be of benefit to all who desire a more substantive spiritual formation. They reflect a Catholic perspective on several vital elements in the formation of character. I believe that they have something to offer anyone who is searching spiritually. They are written in nontechnical language so as to be accessible to all.

Forming our character demands that we acknowledge that there are standards. Growth to maturity comes in realizing that we personally are not the ultimate arbiters of what is right. In coming to maturity, we move beyond the legal minimums to conform ourselves to higher standards. These challenge us to put aside our self-centered ways of thinking and acting. They call us to be our best selves.

For the Christian, the standard is Jesus Christ and his teaching. We seek to live our lives in his Spirit and with his help. Thus we begin our work with some reflections on the role of the Holy Spirit in our spiritual lives.

I. Living in the Spirit

Christians seem to have become more aware recently of the Holy Spirit's presence and activity in their midst. Do the following sound familiar?

> "I wasn't sure what to say, so I prayed to the Holy Spirit to help me find the right words."

> "It was a tough time for all of us, but the Holy Spirit really gave us the strength to pull through."

> "I felt emotionally battered, but gradually the Spirit healed me and I experienced a kind of peace."

People *do* have experiences of God breaking into their lives and increasingly they identify these experiences with the Holy Spirit, the third person of the Trinity. At other times, people refer to this as the action of God's grace. In reality, the Spirit brings grace into our hearts.

How do we experience the Spirit as alive in our midst? It happens in a number of ways, for example:

1. As *wisdom*—not necessarily as the last or most profound word on a subject, but rather as the Spirit leading us to the appropriate word or action at the appropriate time.

2. As *empowerment*—When we are most aware of our human weaknesses and limitations, the Spirit gives us the courage to endure, to transcend our human condition with a newfound strength. Our development of a Christian

character is not merely through our own efforts but in the power of the Spirit.

3. As *openness*—to people, to ideas, to new ways of seeing reality and seeing beyond reality. It is the Spirit who goes before us into the future, who prompts us to dream and to envision.

4. As *freedom*—not freedom as the world defines it, as the multiplication of choices, but the genuine freedom that comes in knowing and doing God's will. The Spirit guides us in "choosing well." The Spirit gives us the clarity to see what is "the right thing to do" and the resolve to carry it out.

5. As *healing*—the grace of the Spirit can heal the deepest problems, sins and griefs in our lives. In a violent world the Spirit brings reconciliation and peace.

The Spirit inspires us to apply Jesus' teaching in practical ways in our everyday lives. Jesus tells us to love our neighbor; the Spirit moves us to visit an elderly aunt in the nursing home, to volunteer at the soup kitchen, to listen to a discouraged child. Jesus gave us the general principles; the Spirit shows how they apply in the specific circumstances of our own lives. The Spirit is rightly linked with the Christian practice of discernment, through which we seek to know and do God's will and thus grow in holiness.[1]

We know that the Spirit dwells among us. Jesus promised that he would remain with us until the end of time, and he kept his promise by sending us his Spirit to be with us. The Spirit guides us, both as individuals and as the people of God, the church. Our personal discernment of God's will occurs in a community which cherishes both Scripture and Tradition as past and present expressions of the guidance of the Spirit.

Ironically, we often recognize the Spirit's work only in

retrospect. When Pope John XXIII called for the Second Vatican Council, many expressed doubts over what it would accomplish. Some wondered if it should be convened at all. Now the Council is generally recognized as the work of the Spirit, a gift to a church that needed to proclaim its message in new ways for the modern world.

As individuals, too, we can look back and see the Spirit's guidance in our lives: the job offer that was accepted or rejected; the friendship that started tentatively but then grew in mutual love for each other and for God; the commitment that was honored even in times of doubts and struggles. These experiences emphasize the need for faith, faith that the Spirit is working to turn all things to the good. This faith should give us a certain optimism and confidence, even when our situation looks bleak and God seems to be absent from our lives.

The Spirit Speaks to Us in Relationships

While the Spirit can and does speak directly to our hearts, we know that the Spirit also speaks through other people and situations.[2] Through the ages, Christians have consulted spiritual directors, confessors and spiritual friends to help them discern what God is saying in their lives. At times, these friends can see us much more clearly than we see ourselves. They can call us to a deeper maturity in response to the Spirit.

Less formally, most of us have, at times, recognized God speaking to us in the words of a colleague, friend—or even an antagonist! And we've also served as the vehicles for bringing God's word to others. Recently a friend casually mentioned that she had received a tentative job offer. I encouraged her to take the offer seriously. A few days later she thanked me for the advice and reported that she had indeed accepted the job and was pleased with her decision. She added that she might have dismissed the offer had I not urged her to think about it.

Living in the Spirit transforms our relationships. They focus outward. We become more concerned with others' well-being than our own. We put our talents and gifts more at the service of others. We see that the gifts given to us by God are for others. Our relationships become more characterized by concern for the spiritual growth of our friends than for our own comfort or control.

The setting for these transformed relationships is often a community, especially a Christian community whose members are committed to discerning and following God's will. If the Spirit speaks to us through others, especially those others who form the Christian community, then we need to participate in that community as actively committed members. It is here that we might most readily hear God's call. Moreover, our relationships with others may—often to our surprise— be critical to their spiritual growth.

Friends in communities nourish and support us. They can sometimes see our latent talents and urge us to use them. A supportive word may be all the encouragement we need to go back to school or to take a new position or to develop a gift for religious education.

Nourishing Maturity in the Spirit

Others can call us beyond our present preoccupations to a deeper spiritual maturity. A group of priests challenged the late Cardinal Bernardin of Chicago not to be so overwhelmed by his administrative duties that he neglected his spiritual life. Subsequently he rose an hour earlier each day to pray before work began.[3] Often just the example of a particularly prayerful friend calls us to reexamine our own life of prayer.

To respond to the Spirit, we need to take some quiet time to think and to pray. A time for regular and sustained prayer is a must if we are to respond effectively during the day to the guidance of the Spirit.

The Spirit also guides us in our ordinary, everyday actions. Jesus promised to be with us always, through his Spirit. All of our actions, even if seemingly insignificant, can be done under the Spirit's power. The Holy Spirit accepts our daily actions, performed in loving obedience to God's will, and makes us holy through them. Even a small act of kindness, done reluctantly in the Spirit, can have surprising results.

A friend shared this incident with me:

> Last spring I made a one-day visit to Cleveland on business. My appointments had finished early, and I slipped into the cathedral for some quiet time. A shabbily dressed older man—a street person, I assumed—came over to me. "Oh, no," I thought. "He wants a handout." So I gave him a dollar and hoped he would go away. He thanked me profusely, collected a few more dollars from other prayers, and left. But then a few minutes, later, I felt him standing behind me. And I smelled what he was holding out—a fresh, hot pizza. "Would you care for a slice, Ma'am?" he asked. I was astonished. With all my experience of urban life, I had never encountered anything like this—a homeless person sharing his bounty with someone who hoped he would disappear. He had gathered up our small individual gifts and turned them into something better.

The Spirit can work in such unexpected ways! Scripture gives several examples, such as Mary's conception of Jesus through the power of the Spirit, or the apostles' amazingly bold preaching after Pentecost.[4] Most of us could probably cite examples in our own lives. These times are infrequent and unpredictable, but they happen often enough to remind us that God alone is in control.

They help us to realize that while we are called every day to work hard toward spiritual and moral growth, only God will bring about its fullness, at a time and by means of his choosing.

> This is by reason of the Holy Spirit who, "dwelling in our hearts by charity" does these works in us, for us, and with us with such exquisite art that these very works which are wholly ours are still more wholly his.[5]

This expectation calls us to a confident hope in God, the transcendent God whose ways are unsearchable.

Living in the Spirit

St. Francis de Sales compares our cooperation with the Spirit to sailing a ship. We have to do our part: load the supplies, set the course and run up the sails, while the Spirit provides the energy, puts the wind in our sails, providing the means to reach our goal.

Much of our sailing is done with the help of others. Recently my youngest niece began to learn people's names. At a family Christmas celebration, my sister and her husband told my niece who everyone was, and she would repeat the names and point to the persons. She even got to know "Uncle John"! Little does she know that these family members will have a great impact on her initial outlook and attitudes in life. Relationships with family members and friends help to form us. Often the Spirit works through these relationships to guide us. Often another person says something we really need to hear.

In the remainder of this book we will look at what we need to do to come to Christian maturity. As we look at ourselves we see that we are already formed in many ways. Yet our character is far from completely "set." Our formation is "ongoing." To grow, we need to learn more. Knowledge can help us to go deeper in our spiritual life. The following chapters will seek to provide some knowledge that can help in this continuing formation of ourselves, our relationships and our communities.

The perspective guiding this effort is that of an attempt to develop some elements of a sound and holistic faith. A young writer notes that:

> Committed Catholics on both the left and the right need to realize that their squabbles are of little help to young people who are searching for solid faith....The church in this country would do well to come together and work out a holistic, traditionally sound legacy to pass on to future generations.[6]

Of course the search for a traditionally sound spiritual legacy is not limited to Catholics. Many Christians yearn for a deeper understanding of faith in the midst of a secularized world. And many other people are searching for meaning in life. The attempt here will be to provide some solid provisions for the ship, realizing that the Holy Spirit is ultimately the one who makes our spiritual sailing possible.[7]

We turn now to a special collection of books written under the guidance of the Holy Spirit. The holy Bible, the Christian Scriptures, provides us with a firm grounding for faith.

QUESTIONS FOR REFLECTION AND DISCUSSION

1. How have you (or haven't you) experienced the Holy Spirit working in your life?

2. What relationships or situations have influenced your spiritual formation up to this point in your life?

II. Studying and
Praying the Scriptures

I will always remember a man who gave us his personal witness to Jesus. I was standing in a crowded subway car early one morning on my way to a meeting. As we entered the downtown area, a fellow passenger got up and addressed the sleepy crowd. He told us briefly of his life of addiction and how he had met Jesus. He quoted a few Scripture passages, invited us to his church next Sunday and then got out at the next stop. His enthusiasm was palpable. The Bible obviously meant a great deal to him, as it had saved his life. While I certainly wouldn't choose his method of sharing his convictions with a captive audience, I admire his commitment to the Gospel.

As with this young man, God speaks to us very specially through Scripture. The Spirit-inspired word of the Bible is a privileged source of divine communication. God can literally change our lives through the holy word. Yet such a radical conversion is a beginning, not an end. It leaves us with a lot to learn. For Scripture must be studied thoroughly to be understood; its meaning is not always obvious. We live in a time quite different from the biblical times. And this immediately leads us to consider the interpretation of Scripture.

Today there is a great deal of debate about fundamentalist and critical approaches to interpreting the words of Scripture. This is an important concern for our spiritual growth. If we are to form our character and make our decisions according to Scripture, we must know what the Bible meant in its time, and what it means for us today.

Scriptural interpretation is a major concern and interest of our times. Some people whom we see these days seem never to be without their Bibles. They read them; they quote them; they try to live them. Sometimes they share a biblical passage with us or challenge us. Many seem to take the Scriptures quite literally.

Once we begin to read the Bible ourselves, we may be similarly enthused. The Scriptures can be fascinating. Not only do they contain God's inspired word, but they speak to our real humanity. From Adam and Eve to Jesus' healing miracles, the Bible offers graphic pictures of the good and the evil in the human condition.

The Bible is appealing in its own right, but we ask ourselves more specifically how it relates to our growth in faith. How do the Scriptures speak to us about how to live? I contend that they do so in a variety of ways.

One common way that I personally experience is the conviction that God is speaking to me in a specific passage. The passage leaps out of the page at me. It provides a new insight or calls for some immediate action. God seems to have spoken to me personally and directly. For instance, in reading a passage in Paul's letter to the Philippians (2:6–11), I know that God is calling me to generous service to others and to a self-emptying in imitation of Christ.

This passage is calling me to go deeper in my spiritual life. The experience is personal. I wouldn't proclaim it to the entire community gathered on Sunday as absolutely necessary for *them*. In fact, I want to compare *my* understanding with the sense of the community. I also have shared the passage with friends to get a different perspective and further insight. In light of this sharing, I seek to live the passage more deeply. I return to it regularly in reflection on my experience of success and failure in generous service.

Scripture also speaks to us through our church communities. Biblical quotations and allusions fill the formal prayers of the church and its sacramental celebrations. Scripture, for example, is inseparable from the Catholic celebration of the eucharist.[1] Church buildings in their art and architecture reflect the basic biblical teachings visually. The church's works of mercy manifest a biblical concern for those in need. In these and many other ways, the church community takes its life from the scriptural teachings.

The Catholic community has some public reflections on the use of Scripture and the variety of ways it speaks to us. Vatican II's Dogmatic Constitution on Divine Revelation *(Dei Verbum)*, for instance, devotes four chapters to Scripture.[2] These reflections call us beyond our personal religious experiences to look at the Scriptures in a critical way so as to understand them more clearly and let them transform our minds and hearts. These reflections remind us that the interpretation of Scripture occurs not just personally but within the community of faith.

Interpretation of the Bible

We seek to interpret the Bible correctly so that we might follow its teaching more faithfully. We seek to understand the Scripture so that we might live more in its spirit. Thus before we can use Scripture, we must understand some ideas that lead us toward faithful interpretation.

The Scriptures are God's inspired word as humanly expressed. They are inspired by the Holy Spirit. This inspiration is not a dictation but grace at work in the hearts of the writers. They give us God's word, but refracted through their human talents and gifts and deficiencies.

The books of the Bible were written in different places and under a variety of circumstances. The words used by the authors are time-conditioned. We need to seek their true meaning since meanings change over time, and we are two thousand or more years distant from the originals.

Thus even those of us who are inexperienced need to be aware of the disciplined, expert interpretation of the text, referred to technically as exegesis. Here we pay attention to the meaning of the words as best we can determine by drawing on ancient texts. We seek to see a passage in light of its total context in the book of which it is a part.

In interpreting, we also look to the literary form of the text. Is the passage a historical incident, a poem, an instructive story or some other literary genre? If we miss the literary form, we may misinterpret the meaning of the passage or book.

For example, if one were to take the story of Jonah literally, we might want to look for the whale capable of swallowing him. On the other hand, if we see that the story is an allegory of the hard-heartedness of the Israel of his time, personified by Jonah, then we look for the intended spiritual meaning. The Ninevites, although pagans, repented at Jonah's reluctant preaching, whereas he continually complained about God's mercy to them. There was a lesson here for Israel, but there is one for us as well.

The literal sense of the passage, the sense originally intended by the author, is the basis for our interpretation. Our search for the literal sense keeps us focused on the text, but not in an inordinate way. Catholics agree with many of our Protestant friends in taking the words themselves very seriously. We part ways at times from our friends of more literalist or fundamentalist inclinations in looking very carefully at the literary form and context of a given passage. Thus we do not literally "turn the other cheek," believing that Jesus was teaching by exaggeration here, but we do agree with the underlying attitude of forgiveness that he was conveying to us. Our concern is to be faithful to Jesus' teaching and to understand it as best we can.

We move from the literal sense to the *sensus plenior*, the deeper meaning of the passage not necessarily intended by the author but intended by God's plan. This comes to the fore in light of further revelation. For example, Job did not believe in eternal life, but Christians do. We look at the Book of Job in light of the further revelation in Jesus Christ. We believe that the Book of Job offers tremendous consolation and insight at times of personal tragedy, but we view its teaching in the context of the Resurrection of Jesus and eternal life.

To grasp the deeper meaning of individual passages or books, we as a community look to the whole of the Scriptures. We interpret the books of the Jewish Scriptures in the light of the coming of Christ. The early Christians looked at their Jewish heritage in this light.

Likewise, we believe that the Bible is a whole and should be viewed as such. The divine revelation is consistent, although our understanding of it will always be inadequate. Yes, there are tensions and different emphases among the various books of the New Testament, but we believe in their basic unity. They are God's word to us, which we can always strive to understand more fully. We will never synthesize the disparate emphases and teachings of Scripture completely, since there is a certain mystery to Scripture that will never be resolved this side of eternity.

We seek to look at the whole and thus to understand the parts. A passage is part of a chapter, which is part of a book of the Scriptures. The book is part of the whole of the scriptural revelation. Thus it is important for us to see passages in context. We are cautious about memorizing or quoting individual passages torn from their context lest they be misunderstood.

Critical analyses and attempts at synthesis are the work of theologians and biblical scholars. Those of us who are less proficient rely on the commentaries, which unfold the riches of the biblical word to us.[3] In our church life, we have embraced a critical understanding of the Scriptures. We understand this as the best contemporary method to get at the real meaning of the Bible so that we can believe and live as God has taught us. If a better method were to be discovered, we would embrace it!

Scriptural Formation of Character

In studying Scripture and seeking to absorb its meaning, we form our hearts and our actions by its instructions. The Bible teaches us how to live.

We can see the scriptural teaching, especially with regard to the New Testament, as embracing both general themes and specific demands. In general, the themes of the Bible form our minds. As we meditate on them and study them, these teachings help us to see the world in a Christian way. When we walk past the homeless person in the street, we ask ourselves if we are the Levite or the priest who walked by in the parable of the Good Samaritan.

As we read and pray the Scriptures both privately and communally, they form our way of looking at things. We see the issues of the day in light of the inspired teachings, especially those given to us by Jesus and the early Christian community. We form our relationships with others in light of the mutual respect and love called for by Christian charity. Our personal sensitivities gradually—though never completely—conform to scriptural teaching.

If we intend to form our mind in Christ, we need to be

attentive to specific teachings of the inspired word. These can be challenging and at variance with the preferences of our secular society. The Sermon on the Mount (Mt 5–7) presents us with arduous and specific directions for living that do not stress material prosperity. The stricture against divorce (Mk 10:2–12), which scholars believe is an authentic teaching of Jesus, causes great difficulty to our contemporary mind-set, which condones easy divorce. While it might be easier for us to dismiss the specific teachings of Scripture on stealing or sex as hopelessly out of date, our mature reflection shows that these challenging teachings are precisely the ones we need to form our Christian character.

As a community, we believe that the Holy Spirit guides us through history, and we come to a deeper understanding of God's will for us over the centuries. But this will does not contradict the scriptural teaching though it may go beyond it or fulfill it. The general directions and specific teachings of the Scriptures, especially the New Testament, are something we must take with the utmost seriousness. They can be challenging to us as a community and as individuals. Historically, we as a church have failed many times to live up to these teachings. But we do not believe that our personal or communal sin invalidates them.

It is critical for us, then, to let the Scriptures challenge our preconceived understandings. The secular world is not something outside us, but rather it is part of us. Our culture influences all Americans in manifold ways. We are primed to reject some scriptural teachings, such as those on social justice, because the modern secular world opposes them. Our task is to let the Scriptures challenge our presuppositions and preunderstandings. Our commitment to Christ engenders an ongoing dialogue of our life with the gospel message embodied in Scripture.

This dialogue is necessary in that we all need to grow in

scriptural principles. Our forgetfulness calls for reminders, and our experience of life calls for deeper reflection. Biblical passages and books speak to us differently at different phases of our lives. They hit home more at one phase of life than at another. Critical life experiences such as the birth of a child, a family wedding or the death of a close family member often enable a particular scriptural incident such as the Nativity, the marriage feast at Cana or the Crucifixion to speak more clearly to us.

Reading the Scriptures is continual nourishment for our spiritual and moral lives. The Scriptures are fundamental for our growth in faith.

Besides studying the Scriptures, we also need to pray the Scriptures. Otherwise our spiritual growth may go on only "in our heads." Many years ago, I taught a student who always got an A on his tests in religion. Yet he had lost his faith and didn't believe the words he wrote. He was not open to discussion and eventually left our Catholic school. He knew about the faith but he did not have faith.

Our knowledge of Scripture is not to be solely intellectual. We meditate on the books of the Bible, seeking to form our minds in them more fully. We imagine the scenes of Scripture, the feelings of the people involved, the healing touch of Jesus, and let our hearts be moved. God draws us and moves us by the inspired word. In prayer, the Scriptures speak to our entire being. At times, they speak to us very personally. They urge us to reach out to others. They provide both norms and directions for life and challenge us to be most fully human in imitation of Christ.

We experience the Scriptures in our communal prayer. We hear them read at our public celebrations. We listen to priests and ministers expound on their meaning and their application to our daily lives. In our religious communities and our families, we also see the good example of others.

While we often note our communal inadequacies in following Christ, it is also good to look around to see the many splendid efforts others are making to follow him, to live his word. On Sunday in church, we can see adult children who make considerable efforts to bring their elderly parents to the celebration. We can see around us those whom we know are making special efforts to visit the sick or attend to the dying.

The example of others can lead us to a deeper life of prayer and to a sensitivity to God's presence with us. The example of others often leads us to that love and respect for humanity that the Bible enjoins. A life shaped by the study of Scripture yields that sensitive respect for human dignity to which we now turn.

QUESTIONS FOR REFLECTION AND DISCUSSION

1. Has Scripture helped to form you as a person? How?

2. How do you go about interpreting Scripture?

3. Does Scripture have a role in your moral decision making?

III. Personal Growth
in Community

$\mathcal{P}$resident Bush's phrase, "a kinder, gentler America," struck a responsive chord in Americans who listened to his 1988 inaugural address. To Americans weary of incivility and violence, he held out the ideal of mutual respect and charity. In religious terms, such concerns for one another rest on the intrinsic dignity and worth of the human person—the personal subject of inalienable rights to "life, liberty and the pursuit of happiness."

Respect for human dignity is critical to spiritual and moral growth. Such respect has deep roots in Christianity. The Genesis account of the creation of the world refers to male and female being created in the image and likeness of God (Gen 1:27). Christians believe that the coming of Christ restored human dignity. Jesus' life, richly portrayed in the Scriptures, shows us the fullness of what it means to be human while he redeems us from our slavery to original and personal sin. The Holy Spirit, sent by Jesus, enables us to live out the fullness of our spiritual gifts.

Thinkers have meditated on human dignity for centuries. For example, one constant theme in the writings of St. Francis de Sales (1567–1622) is the dignity of the human person. We will take a few moments to explore the meaning of human dignity in de Sales's thought. He is representative of the best of the Catholic spiritual tradition on this key reality.[1]

19

Made in God's Image

For St. Francis de Sales, the human person as made in God's image is basically a loving person. God is a Trinity of persons—Father, Son and Holy Spirit—in constant loving communication with each other. The Trinity is a community of love. Made in God's image, each human person is drawn to communication with other persons, is made for community, and is happiest in union with God.

Just as God's love "reaches out" in creating and sustaining our magnificent universe and our humanity, so too humans reach out in love to others. We are like the infant who stretches out its arms to its mother. Love keeps infants alive. Tragically, infants can literally die if deprived of love. And we are quite well aware that adults can die too for lack of love—though not so obviously.

In the human person, there is a longing for God.[2] This is evident in all civilizations. Christians believe that the loving Other to whom humans are most deeply directed is Christ. Jesus is the ultimate goal who gives purpose to all creation. We can only attain our full humanity in friendship with him. The Gospel of Christ is not extrinsic to the person but fulfills his or her deepest longings.

We are made in the image of God. What more can we say about this? First of all, we can say that we are made to love as God loves. There is dynamism and movement in our essential being. We are not made to be inert but active. In this activity, we can degrade ourselves in sin or rise to holiness in imitation of Christ. We can model ourselves on Mother Teresa or Machiavelli; we can selfishly accumulate possessions or we can share them generously; we can aid those in need or act only for ourselves.

Second, we can say that self-love is appropriate. We are reflections of the Trinity. We are called to love ourselves and appreciate the talents and gifts we have. We are valuable individuals in God's eyes. We have much for which to give thanks.

Third, we can say that humans are made for community. By loving others, we can help them to grow in the divine image. The soul not only realizes the image of God in itself by acting in love toward the neighbor, but also stimulates the neighbor to grow in likeness to God by loving in return. There is a reciprocal effect here that builds the Christian community. The loving image of God comes to full fruition in that community which is the church.

There a mutuality between God and the human person. Our indigence is best filled by God's bountifulness. The foregoing considerations, based on the writings of St. Francis de Sales, show us an essential optimism about human nature and the fullness that loving God brings.

This is not to say that the effects of sin are not profound. Our will, in which lies our ability to love, is greatly weakened by sin. Our reason too is obviously distorted by sin. Our present-day experience confirms these effects of sin. How often do we love manipulatively rather than genuinely; how often do we rationalize our denial of human rights; how often do we accept the killing of the unborn or the elderly or the handicapped? We readily deny responsibility for our own violence.

Even after the fall of Adam and Eve, the basic human inclination toward God remains but can be truly fulfilled only in the gracious love given to humanity by the incarnate Christ. God communicates with humanity in the Son, and this communication continues to the present day in the Holy Spirit. Only in this friendship with God will the soul's deepest longings be fulfilled and the effects of sin be mitigated.

Living Gently

As we grow spiritually, the loving image of God comes to fruition within us. Gradually we become more and more virtuous. All moral virtues, each in its particular way, are manifestations of love. One virtue that has particular relevance in our day and is in particular need of being developed is gentleness.

A gentle person treats every other person, no matter how flawed, disfigured, or sinful, as worthy of respect. Thus the gentle person acts with great civility toward others because such civility is a sign of respect for the dignity of the person.

The gentle person does not use offensive language or talk down to others. Rather he or she uses words to encourage, support and affirm others in their life and work. Gentle people realize that speech creates a certain kind of human community. "Talking trash" creates an atmosphere disrespectful of others.

The gentle person really listens to the other—even at great length—and seeks to understand him or her. The gentle person does not leap to conclusions, but seeks first to understand. The gentle person, while sometimes challenging another's views, seeks not to forget the basic worth of the other person in the dialogue.

Gentleness calls for a continued growth in self-knowledge, not merely for self-fulfillment, but that we might share our gifts more effectively with others. Since violence and incivility are not just around us—in crime, musical lyrics and offensive expressions of "individual rights"—but are within us, we need to seek out the sources of our own anger, our own outbursts of crude language, our own incivility. Gentleness toward others comes out of an inner discipline which builds on self-understanding.

Gentleness requires courage. It takes courage to face ourselves and work at changing the uncivil self; it takes courage to respect those who differ exceedingly from ourselves. The courage in gentleness lies in standing up in civil society for the common good and for simple decency when these are disdained. The courage in gentleness is in working nonviolently to transform unjust social structures.[3] A "kinder, gentler America" is one with the courage of its convictions about human dignity.

Families Are the Basic Community

As we have seen, human beings grow best in a loving environment. Respect for human dignity calls us to build that environment. Children in particular grow in response to care. "The authority of the parents can be exercised properly only when...it fosters the physical and moral growth of the child."[4]

The core community that forms us to respect ourselves and others is the family. When families are denigrated or deemed dispensable, children suffer. Intact and loving two-parent families are best for the well-being of children and the well-being of adults as well. At their best, parents carefully teach self-discipline and self-restraint. In taking responsibility, they teach responsibility. In loving generously, they teach love.

> The truth is that every child needs and deserves the love and provision of a mother and a father. The loving two-married-parent family is the best environment for children—the place where children gain the identity, discipline, and moral education that are essential for their full individual development. And, as the institution that most effectively teaches the civic virtues of honesty, loyalty, trust, self-sacrifice, personal responsibility and respect for others, the family is an irreplaceable foundation for long-term social efficacy and responsibility.[5]

Such loving families still exist and still perform generous works of charity out of the limelight. Yet social com-
mentators note with alarm the weakening of marriage.
Fatherless families are quite common in our civil society,
and personal (sexual) expression seems to have replaced
the old-fashioned idea of self-sacrifice and commitment.[6]
To some, fathers seem to be dispensable, but of course
they aren't.[7]

> ...creating such a family and keeping it intact have become
> increasingly difficult; the communities of support for the
> family have weakened, and many family functions have
> been taken over by the economy and the state. As a result,
> the component parts of the nuclear family ideal have begun
> to drift apart....[8]

The family, now the place of personal satisfaction rather
than one centered on the upbringing of children, often
falls to divorce. The rise of a "divorce culture" challenges
the prevalence of marriage. Here marriage is for personal
satisfaction. Yet the need for satisfaction expands infi-
nitely. No human relationship can satisfy that infinite
longing for satisfaction that can be fulfilled only in God.
Long ago St. Augustine, no stranger to the search for personal fulfillment, said that "Our hearts are restless 'til they
rest in Thee."

Preference for the intact and loving two-parent family
should not blind us to the fact that family life cannot
always be maintained. In cases of domestic violence or
drug or alcohol abuse, the well-being of the victimized
spouse and children can require that the abuser be separated from the family. Even when violence and abuse are
not present, other issues, such as the self-indulgence
mentioned above, can severely strain a marriage. Couples
can be encouraged to seek counseling or to seek assistance from "Retrouvaille" or similar groups who work

with troubled marriages. If a divorce occurs, the under-standing and support of a loving community can be vital, especially for newly single parents who are learning to raise children alone.

Renewing the Family

Renewal of the family is now being sought through per-sonal and societal conversion. There are calls to re-create a "marriage culture." A return to our religious and civic roots seems to be the only way to heal our problems. Parents need to be convinced that commitment precedes pleasure; fathers need to be convinced that their presence is indis-pensable for their children's well-being. This attitude is really a matter of a change of heart. No external imposition can create a personal commitment. It comes from within the person—though it can be facilitated by the example, concern and challenge of others and by a society and a gov-ernment that encourage marital commitment.

From the Catholic point of view, marriage is a relation-ship of mutuality. Both husband and wife have to work at it with energy and sensitivity. Its life is really made possible in Christ. Only in the grace of the Holy Spirit can marriage achieve its fullness; only with hard work in cooperation with this grace can it succeed.

A recently widowed friend once told me that it was the grace of marriage that was her sustaining force in dealing with her husband's prolonged ill health. She couldn't have continued without God's help.

Marriage needs community support. If this is not found in the wider secular community, then it can be in a smaller circle of friends. These are circles of people who similarly value marriage. They provide a positive environment—not just of values but of activities and of humor. Nights out together with children at a ball game, trips to the beach and other ordinary but important activities characterize these communities of mutual support.

Such friends can be someone to turn to when people at the supermarket give parents dirty looks for having two or three children. Friends can be supportive when parents encounter that cultural and business climate that discourages family life in favor of career advancement, personal satisfaction or profit.

At their best, families sustain those in need through service. I have friends who took in Vietnamese refugees after the war to help them get settled in this country. Others make a regular practice of visiting the elderly in nursing homes. Parental good example helps children to develop their own sense of responsibility.

A friend recently shared this example from her life:

> When thinking of family as the first community that we experience, I recall my own childhood and the lessons I learned of how to live and serve the larger community. My grandparents did not have much in the way of material possessions during the Great Depression, but their door was always open to those in need. I remember folks coming to their door at all hours of the day and night for food, clothing and even a little money at times for some emergency. These were the days before the welfare system, and my grandparents felt the responsibility of caring for their neighbors.[9]

The task at hand is to re-create values and attitudes for the future. There is no sense lamenting the demise of the family culture of a few decades ago. The task before us is to build a family-friendly environment among like-minded friends in our neighborhoods and civic communities and in our government. We need to re-create the bias that favors family stability over family dissolution.

An element that strongly affects efforts to build family life is the electronic media. Many of us grew up with television and consider it a customary and necessary part of our homes. Our eyes are drawn to the television like a magnet.

Several years ago an acquaintance of mine announced at a spirituality conference that she and her husband had decided *not* to have a television in their home. This decision was somewhat to the consternation of their children—and to the participants at the conference! She felt that if they ever really needed a television, they could rent one.

Her deeper point was that television brings a variety of attitudes right into homes, often with little thought given to their impact. The secular values of the mainstream media dominate television. We become accustomed to these values through repetition. They especially affect children if they have no counterweight through discussion with parents. Just as with adults, the environment affects children. But children lack the broader life perspective that helps adults to evaluate what they see and hear.

I believe that technology can work to strengthen ties as well as weaken them. Families today can keep in touch through electronic mail as well as through the telephone. One couple I know communicates with their son in Hong Kong through E-mail. Others hear regularly from their children at college in the same way. Good television programs can bring families together for the evening.

We should note that the experience of younger adults is different than those of us in midlife and beyond. For many in Generation X, the divorce of their parents has been a painful reality. For this generation, the sexual revolution was a fact of life as they grew up. Their task was to deal with sexual freedom, not sexual restraints.[10] The concomitant breakdown of families and communities did not help them in the process of adjustment.

In previous generations, a strong family structure and a vibrant religious culture could provide much-needed support and call social norms into question. Now the family is weaker and the Catholic culture of the past is fast disappearing. We have reached the point where a vital new culture needs to emerge. We will have to work more conscientiously at creating a family-friendly environment.

The family is the primary community for religious formation. Here children first encounter religious culture and moral principles. They learn that we are a religious community gathered in Christ's name. They learn from parents how to evaluate what they see on television or in life. Neighboring abortion clinics, gay couples or industrial polluters provide real opportunities for discussion of Catholic moral teaching and respect for human dignity. The balance to the surrounding secular pragmatism lies in a knowledge of moral principles and their sensitive application.

We are called to such support and sharing with one another in our families and communities. This can be most often in ordinary things. A critical issue for many families these days is finding time to be together. Both parents and children have busy schedules. One family I know schedules a "family night" each week so they can be together!

Small Groups as Community

A person who truly respects human dignity continually seeks to understand Christian community, both in the family and in the "intentional" community—more deeply. She or he seeks to enhance that community, with the help of God's grace, so that a gentle love may flourish and prosper. Such Christian communities will need to continue to reach out to build a civil society that respects human dignity and curbs oppression and injustice. Work to overcome the evil of racism, for example, would be one element in our efforts to build a gentle and just society.

One major influence on communal life today is the growth of small groups. Overall, this has been a quite positive development in our culture. Robert Wuthnow has made an extensive study of the strengths and weaknesses of these groups. He "...argues that the small-group movement is beginning to alter American society, both by changing our understandings of community and by redefining spirituality."[11] Here God is less an external reality and more of an internal presence. God is a God who can relate to us personally. The danger we must guard against is reducing God to ourselves—making God in our image. This can be done if we keep in mind the multiplicity of ways—through Scripture, Tradition, personal inspirations, friends, nature and so forth—that God speaks to us.

Four out of ten Americans belong to small groups. Sometimes these groups replace churches, though more often they tend to be affiliated with churches. Wuthnow says that small groups allow us to bond easily but also to break our attachments easily. They do not substitute for commitment to family and the church with its doctrine and standards.

A small group is not a family. Yet for many people, small groups are sources of the emotional support that all of us need. But groups are not the same as the ongoing challenges and constraints of family life. If you belong to a group and don't like where it is heading, you can just stop going to the meetings. It is more difficult to leave a family. We don't control family life in the same way we can control our membership in a small group. Families ultimately call for a more mature interaction.

In our country, small groups tend to focus more on the God of security than on the God of justice. "It is more aptly conceived as an orientation that encourages a safe, domesticated version of the sacred."[12] These groups can take the challenge out of church life. Ultimately they do not prove useful unless they bring us out of our cultural tendency toward self-preoccupation.

One issue related to preoccupation with self is: what we get out of groups versus what we put in. Many small groups focus on encouragement and personal growth. And frankly, many of us need this encouragement in times of grief, stress and transition. Life can be very difficult, and sometimes the best we can do is to "hang in there" with a little help from our friends.

Yet for true growth, one must go beyond affirmation from others to sharing one's talents and gifts even without hope of return. A vibrant Christian community evangelizes; it shares its faith with others. The first task is to live like Christ, and immediately this brings us into contact with others. Love reaches out—it is not selfish.

Small groups are helpful for those in the throes of a transition such as divorce, who need ongoing help with addictions or who want to pray together. They can form base communities for those who are reaching out to share faith with others. They provide places to get support, share new ideas, and reflect on experience. Essentially, small groups are good, but as with any good thing, they have some dangers.

Renewing the Civic Community

The wider civic community can help to safeguard and nourish human dignity and the formation of character. It can either support or challenge our basic principles. Recently some have called for a renewal of the civil community. They argue that just as there are individual rights and responsibilities, there are communal rights and responsibilities.[13]

For example, what are "the rights of the community" (traditional Catholicism would say the *common good*) in regard to the use of public spaces? Must these spaces be ceded to the homeless? "While it is certainly true that all individuals, including the homeless, do have the right to use public areas, it is also true that the general public has a similar right to safe, clean, and peaceful public spaces."[14] All people are called to respect public spaces.

The renewal of community has an institutional dimension. Institutions need to be nourished, for they help to promote the common good. They also help to form the individual's character for better or for worse. Investment of energy in improving institutions is an investment in bettering both individuals and the civil community.

Actually, institutions affect us from the very beginning. Our identity is tied up with them. While the pattern of human growth is toward exercising greater autonomy and taking greater responsibility, we can do so only in the context of institutions such as the family and the school. Autonomy "...is only one virtue among others and...without such virtues as responsibility and care, which can be exercised only through institutions, autonomy itself becomes an empty form without substance."[15] Institutions, with their standards, their accountability, and their calls for responsibility, mold character.

A vibrant civic community is an absolute necessity if human dignity is to be nourished and protected. Neither government nor the market economy itself is able to provide what people really need. Only a healthy community can do so.[16] Local communities are built on the ordinary events of life and on spiritual activities such as prayer or visiting the sick. These do not make news, but they form people.

A language of mutuality, of relationship, needs to modify that of rights in our civic discussions. Rights imply conflict; obligation implies dialogue and mutual concern. We see such a dialogue in the question of homelessness mentioned earlier. Alice S. Baum and Donald Burnes have challenged the civil community to get to the roots of homelessness and begin to deal with the real issues. Arguing from their own experience gained from working with the homeless and from current research, they contend

> ...that up to 85 percent of all homeless adults suffer from chronic alcoholism, drug addiction, mental illness, or some combination of the three, often complicated by serious medical problems.[17]

They argue that we need to get beyond our denial to see the roots of the problem. Then we can look for models that will enable us to deal with homeless people in a way that respects human dignity, restores community and enhances the common good. Some homeless advocates have reservations about Baum and Burnes's stance, but their arguments have focused dialogue on the roots of the problem and how best to respond if we are to be a community.

Caring families, vibrant religious congregations and concerned civil communities are a necessity if we are to come to a deep respect for human dignity, as we mentioned at the beginning of this chapter. We will turn now to some further consideration of the church as a community in which we can form our Christian character and achieve spiritual growth.

QUESTIONS FOR REFLECTION AND DISCUSSION

1. Have you ever belonged to a small group? Can you describe the experience? Was the group beneficial to you? Do you share some of the cautions expressed above?

2. What is your fundamental attitude toward institutions? How did you form this attitude? Do you agree that some institutions are vital for the healthy functioning of civil society?

3. What is your experience of family life? Do you see ways that your family life could be improved?

IV. Believing in the Church Today

$\mathcal{A}$ friend wrote this reflection a few years ago: "The...church is my lifeboat on the sea of life. When in troubled waters I am grateful for its protection and comfort. Only when the waters are calm am I aware of the design deficiencies and need for maintenance of this lifeboat of faith."[1]

The church today is in need of maintenance and support. The church today is in transition. "...[T]he conclusion that we are in the midst of a period of really fundamental change in American religious life is now almost universally conceded."[2] As in the wider secular society, there are many opportunities and problems at this time of change.

As mentioned in the previous chapter, a core question for Americans is whether our spiritual life will be individualistic, reflecting the surrounding ethos of autonomy, or whether it will be truly relational and communal. The thrust of our milieu is toward isolated autonomy. We have a tendency to make our own decisions in light of our needs and self-interest. Today it seems that the sole guiding cultural principle is "to do no harm to others." Recently this relativistic point of view has been called into question by religious leaders, but it is still a powerful force in our society.

A central contention of this book is that we are intrinsically relational, and that excessive individualism strips us of an important aspect of our humanity. Spiritual and moral growth comes in relationships in communities.

Membership in the church community is not just optional for faith—it is essential. Not only does the church follow the

34

Holy Spirit and reverence the Scriptures, but it provides the preeminent place where the spiritual life is lived. In the early decades of church life, the communities in Jerusalem, Corinth, Rome and elsewhere were critical for the development and spread of the Christian faith. We note that in the first centuries of Christianity, the isolated Christian ascetics in the Egyptian desert soon saw the wisdom of banding together into communities. Throughout Christian history, spiritual growth and communal relationships have gone hand in hand. We grow spiritually in relationships. As mere individuals we tend to sink into the ocean of our own self-concern.

The church community calls us out of ourselves. It calls us to serve others. The church community provides limits and it holds us to standards. It challenges us against self-centeredness and our tendency toward a secularized faith of "a little of this and a little of that and nothing too demanding." The church calls us to measure our subjectivity against the truths of human nature and the standards of human dignity.

The vitality of the church as an organized community is important. Institutions carry forward the moral principles and good works that we need to embrace if we are to grow spiritually. Institutions provide a network of continuity that is lost when a work is entrusted to singular individuals who may eventually weary of carrying the burden and retire. I think of some acquaintances who volunteered their time to help the reemerging churches in eastern Europe. As the years wore on, their resources waned, their energies flagged and they had to abandon this good work. I can't help thinking that if they had worked in an institutional framework their good work might even now be carried on by others.

Institutional communities are worth our support. They have long-lasting effects. They care for us in the storms and shipwrecks of life. They help to form and support people.

Church communities have been a major factor in fostering personal relationships and promoting spiritual formation throughout American history. I think of the generations of immigrants, including some of my ancestors, who received spiritual and material support from parishes and religious communities in the nineteenth and twentieth centuries. These communities enabled the immigrants to have long-term success.

In this chapter, I will discuss the church, and in particular the one I know best—the Roman Catholic Church in the United States. I believe that many of my reflections here will be readily transferable to other religious traditions and denominations in the American milieu. I will discuss a few current trends and point to some future directions that might be fruitful for the Catholic Church. In considering the state of the church, I hope that we will see the need to diminish internal strife and strike a better balance in our communal lives. I hope that we will provide a more conducive environment for navigating the spiritual life.

Believing Today

One underlying question of our day is that of faith and our belief in the community of faith, the church. In this era of skepticism regarding institutions, people today are asking themselves what they really believe. People are once again asking religious questions. Religious truths, once banished from the public forum by the priority given to empirical science, are now gradually returning to the public arena in serious discussions (regarding such topics as capital punishment, character formation or the problems of fatherless families, to name a few).

More recently science and philosophy appear no less to be abandoning the Enlightenment's understanding of rationality. It is increasingly admitted that there is no unquestionable starting point for knowledge that stands outside all social and cultural context, all presuppositions formed by traditions and ways of life."[3]

People searching for deeper spiritual meaning in life are freer these days to probe both the rationality and the mystery of belief. Today we recognize that even science has its starting points. There are presuppositions, called *paradigms* in the technical language, that govern scientific inquiry. Such presuppositions are even more evident in the subjective or "soft" sciences such as sociology or psychology. If today's experts are looking at both the reasonableness and social foundations of these "hard" and "soft" sciences, it seems wise for us to look again more deeply at the bases of faith within the Christian community.

Today we are free to join a community of faith and learn of the depths of God's love. A religious tradition can help us to be truly reasonable—to be open to all of reality rather than espouse materialism in a limited scientific sense. We are meant to listen to all the ways that God speaks to us. These include the wonders of atomic physics, the beauty of the sun setting over quiet waters or the example of a compassionate friend caring for an abandoned child. I would contend that faith is reasonable, that it guides us to the mysterious depths of human existence, and that the journey of faith never ends.

American Catholicism in Transition

A prime instance of a community of faith in transition is American Catholicism. The Second Vatican Council (1962–65) and the American cultural upheaval of the 1960s unleashed a series of changes in the Catholic community whose reverberations are still being felt thirty years later.

American Catholicism has changed dramatically. Much of this change has been for the good; some has not. We will concern ourselves with a few aspects of the current situation and their implications for our spiritual lives.

The Catholic community has experienced profound shifts in the last thirty years. One of these is the continuing decline in the number of priests, sisters and brothers and the increase in the number of ecclesial lay ministers.

> At present there are at least 12,000 lay women and men, not including school teachers, employed in U.S. parishes....There are twice as many lay students (about 6,000) pursuing graduate studies in theology and ministry as there are seminarians (about 3,000) in graduate programs.[4]

This renewed appreciation of the lay vocation brings a concomitant reemergence of lay spirituality that is rejuvenating people throughout the community. The lay vocation is lived preeminently in the secular world. Most lay people become spiritually mature in living out their vocation in society—as teachers, office workers, computer programmers, government employees, plumbers and so forth. Integration is key here.

I remember a good friend who returned to the workplace after many years spent raising a family. The strident secular values stunned her. Not one to give up easily, she gradually won her younger coworkers' respect for her Christian approach to others and her honesty in her work. She did precisely what needed to be done—she began to change her environment for the better. She did not park her spiritual life with her car; she brought it into the office. Ultimately the renewal of lay spirituality will be a renewal of our church and civil communities.

The increasing number of lay ministers in the church is making a change, the full implications of which are not yet completely discernible. Change in personnel and the relationships they forge will certainly have an impact on the community in the short and long term. The talents of numerous lay women and men in ministry are coming to the fore. The use of the varied talents of people and the focus on collaboration in church ministry has been very much for the good. The recent Murnion study of ecclesial lay ministry found the presence of more women in church ministry has tended to make parish ministry more "nurturing" than it had been previously.[5] The study also found that the presence of paid, professional lay ministers in a parish seems to increase lay participation in the church.

Since most lay ministers are women, this change in personnel will call on them to become more sensitive to men's characteristic interests and concerns. Reciprocally, there is a need for men in ministry to do the same for women. The ideal is for both men and women to work together, each following his or her vocation, and using their pooled gifts to build up the community and one another.[6]

Internal Divisions

Another characteristic of recent Catholicism is greater participation of community members in the sacraments and other aspects of church life. This participation extends to the eucharistic celebration, where there are diverse participants such as the music minister, the lector and the eucharistic minister. Participation includes everything from sitting on the parish finance council or the parish advisory board to teaching religious education or visiting the sick.

Another side of the more participatory church has been the fracturing of the American church into pressure groups of the "Left" and the "Right." This change has shattered the uniformity of the recent past and created some difficulties.[7]

Here is a new situation for us as a community. We are becoming more like the disparate church of the Middle Ages and less like the church of the centuries prior to Vatican II. This situation is not likely to alter anytime soon.

The models for this change come from the political arena. There are liberals, conservatives and moderates, all with their own agendas for the future of the church, all with supportive publications and theologians. Each group seeks to exert pressure for its own agenda through personal contacts or media relations (or exposés), through protests of various sorts and through conferences with like-minded individuals.

The current state of the church involves a great deal of labeling. Labels for groups or individuals—"liberal" or "conservative," "radical feminist" or "religious rightist"— are samples of the inevitable shorthand that emerges in writing and speaking. Labels also can be obstacles to *listening to* and *learning from* one another. They can become a major preoccupation and keep us from paying attention to God's call to love. A label can keep us from seeing the person as person, and from respecting the dignity of the other enough to listen to what the person really believes and feels, rather than just responding to what his or her label implies.

To truly listen, we need to have some inner personal security and a real respect and zeal for human dignity. It can be threatening to listen to someone with whom we disagree, especially if what the person says makes some sense and calls us to question our own beliefs or prejudices.

One virtue called for in the present situation is humility. Humility is that virtue which enables us to see ourselves as we truly are. Here we neither put ourselves down nor exalt ourselves. We thank God for our talents and gifts, and we acknowledge our weaknesses and deficiencies.

An aspect of humility that needs to come to the fore is the

admission that "I may not be right." The acknowledgment of personal fallibility is a must. Once acknowledged, this fallibility opens us to learn more. Even those who do not agree with us may have more of the truth than we like to admit. Thus it is important to give others a fair hearing. Mutual respect for the dignity of one another should never be lacking if we are to follow the Gospel.

In order to deal with the real conflicts that exist in the church, we need to be self-critical, not just self-congratulatory. We need to forsake our personal infallibility in a search for the truth, which implies that we will continue to deepen our understanding of the mysteries of faith and their implications. Learning occurs in the give-and-take of debate.[8] Hard as it is to admit, the Holy Spirit might actually be guiding our opponent!

This listening to others should involve reading periodicals whose editorial opinion is slanted in a direction which opposes our own thinking. This effort runs counter to our inclination to stay in our niche of agreeable opinions— spending all our time reading and speaking with those we find congenial and who agree with us. This also runs counter to the human tendency, the result of original sin, to blame someone. Adam blamed Eve; Eve blamed the serpent; we blame others. Thus we refuse to take responsibility and to accept the challenges that God gives us to let go of our seeming securities and to be more like Jesus.

The divisions in the church—some say the fragmentations—are calling us to seek a new balance. We are still struggling as a Catholic community with a balance between the "quasi-collectivism" of the 1950s and the individualism of our current culture. What we should strive for is a realistic balance of respect for individual conscience on the one hand and for the importance of the common good/community life on the other. Neither a suffocating collectivism nor a selfish individualism is desirable.

As we emerge from the post-Conciliar era and set our sails for the winds of the twenty-first century, we not only need to deal effectively with our divisions but also to revisit our intellectual, cultural and spiritual roots.

A Community of Faith and Culture

Many lament the breakdown of civility and thoughtfulness in the church. Others note a major concern in the Christian community today. Our younger members have little knowledge of our rich roots in Scripture and Tradition. Many can offer little resistance to our cultural incivility and lack of faith. Their faith is thin. The arguments for faith offered by Augustine, Aquinas, John Henry Newman or even Bishop Fulton Sheen are foreign to them. These great thinkers offer a language, a culture and a way of thinking totally unknown to many. The pervasive secular culture fills the gaps with its own doctrine. Many sincere Catholics espouse a Catholicism formed more by stories in the newsmagazines and the media, with their emphasis on controversial issues and conflict, than by the positive principles, communal solidarity and respect for human dignity guiding Catholicism at its best.

As we saw in the section on interpreting Scripture, our adherence to Christianity and Catholicism in particular is a matter of understanding and intellectual conviction. There is a content to the faith that we need to grapple with and master.[9] Christian faith is emotional but not based on emotion. It is an encounter with the grace of Jesus Christ. This is not solely a personal encounter such as: I met Jesus and he changed my life. Rather, it is also an encounter with Jesus in the content of the faith that he has given us as a community, under the inspiration of the Holy Spirit. We first meet Jesus and encounter his Spirit within a community.

One must come to know the Scriptures and the Spirit-inspired Tradition and their meanings if one is to be a believer who is growing spiritually. If we give our whole selves to Christ, our emotions and our reason must be more and more conformed to him. It is hard work to be Christian. There is always the need to understand things better, to go deeper in grasping the basics of salvation and to broaden the base of our knowledge and commitment. All this takes time and effort.

At the same time, we need to let this knowledge form our actions. There is no true faith without deeds of virtue that spring from a compassionate love for others. However, as we listen to and serve others, new questions arise that propel us back to Scripture and Tradition and to the theological explanations that help us to understand them more fully. The great thinkers and saints, from Paul to Teresa of Avila to Francis de Sales, can help us with their thoughts on the profundity of faith.

True faith, then, is emotional but is also guided by reason; it is an encounter with Jesus personally and intellectually as well as within the community. Christian faith at its best embraces the simplest of believers while it prods the most intellectual to further thought.

Such faith inevitably has its cultural expressions. Strong inner convictions manifest themselves in the life of the believer. If that person happens to be a poet or an artist, then it happens naturally that he or she expresses this religious belief through art or poetry. Christian religious culture seems to be at a low ebb right now. One prominent editor believes that "Over the next decade we must work to reconstitute a viable and vital Catholic culture."[10] If we are to create an integral culture that will transmit faith, then art, music, literature and education must be renewed and take on a new mode of modern religious inspiration.

An intellectual and cultural renewal will call for generosity and commitment. "History shows that church renewal has always come through greater sacrifice, never through less."[11] To renew the church will require a clear vision and dedication to that vision. Renewal groups and movements that call for dedication and sacrifice will prosper, while groups offering no clarity of ministerial commitment or distinct difference from the mores of our age are already faltering.

Renewing the Moral Life

As we move to deepen our personal and communal commitment to Christ, we seek to express that commitment in practical deeds. Thus we come to the great debates today over the content of Christian morality—over what one must do in the contemporary world to live the Christian life. Since the Second Vatican Council called explicitly for a renewal of moral theology,[12] extended debates over moral questions have arisen, and new schools of thought with competing methodologies have emerged.[13]

We now seem to be at a point of respite and reconsideration of these debates. Pope John Paul's 1993 encyclical letter *Veritatis Splendor*[14] (The Splendor of Truth) on moral theology broke no new ground but gave us pause to reconsider the debates. Its main thrust was toward questions of fundamental morality and moral systems.

While more remains to be said, *Veritatis Splendor* merits our careful and prayerful consideration. Its conclusion that certain approaches to morality—such as consequentialism with its emphasis primarily on results—are seriously defective and have "gone overboard" must be taken seriously. The encyclical's thesis is that these approaches should no longer be followed because they do not adequately express a proper Catholic understanding of either moral truth or the demands of the Gospel. While they are well meaning and have certain strengths, ultimately these schools of thought have failed to articulate essential moral elements of Scripture and the Tradition.

Clearly the renewal of moral theology called for by Vatican II remains to be accomplished. If certain approaches have proven to be inadequate, what can we learn from them as we move to a more complete synthesis? The point here is not that we should return to some supposed halcyon age of the past. We need to hear God speaking now. Some efforts have not succeeded; new efforts must be made. Our moral thinking needs to continue to develop.

The future of moral theology lies, I believe, in studying the Christian virtues and asking how one develops into a virtuous person, a spiritually mature person, a person of Christian character. Over the last thirty years, debates have raged over human acts, moral evil and sin. A renewed focus on virtue would emphasize the positive context of our decision making. In infinite love, God calls each of us to holiness. Motivated by love rather than fear, we respond by turning away from sin and toward the good. We begin to reorient our lives.

Turning toward the good and turning our lives over to God is an ongoing process. It is accomplished primarily in prayer. Prayer and moral decision making go together for the mature Christian. Their interrelationship "is a bit of a rediscovery for Catholic moral theology."[15] In the decades prior to the Second Vatican Council, spirituality and morality were studied in isolation from each other. One of the benefits of our attempts to renew moral theology has been the realization of the importance of their connection.

As Christians we come to the virtuous life through our

life of prayer. Prayer is a relationship of dialogue with God. Prayer is ongoing and propels us out of ourselves to others.

Our life of prayer influences our decisions. Ideally we take our decisions to God rather than just making them on our own. Prayer can bring us into a listening mode. Prayer can balance our selfishness with its focus outward. It is in this context that we make our best moral decisions.[16]

Prayer does not replace moral analysis but assists it.

> The person of authentic prayer becomes more—not less— attentive to reason, to laws, and to the wisdom of the Church since each is another path to know God's will more completely and therefore allows the Christian to respond to God more authentically.[17]

The renewal of moral theology as well as the balancing of the competing visions noted earlier will only be accomplished as we grow spiritually, as we grow in virtue.

Virtue grows through our loving responses in everyday situations. We answer God's call to holiness and moral discernment in our ordinary activities—in the home, at work, in the parish, in the community. Virtue ethics speaks the language of love, but not the "mushy" anything-goes love glorified in the media. This love requires commitment, work and, yes, even self-sacrifice, but always in the context of a life-giving relationship with God and one another.[18] This is the love that gives meaning to life, the "fullness of life" that Jesus promised and that is the ultimate goal of the virtuous life.

Our sensitivity to our relationship with God, and our listening, naturally broadens out to others in our environment. Eventually we become aware of those structures that enhance or erode respect for human life.

This transitional period in church life calls for a positive renewal of our moral witness. Focus on good acts and virtuous living can provide a key to developing more adequate moral systems. A positive approach can meet head-on the challenges and opportunities of our time. A strong anchor for this positive approach is the ongoing development of our conscience. We will now set sail for this harbor.

QUESTIONS FOR REFLECTION AND DISCUSSION

1. What is your basic attitude toward the church? What is the origin of this attitude?

2. What has been your experience of ministry in the world and in the church?

3. How do you feel about listening to those who disagree with you? Have you found encounters with others and their views helpful to your spiritual growth and maturity?

V. The Dynamic Christian Conscience

$\mathcal{A}$ most startling aspect of our society is the absence of guilt. Some people kill, rape and abuse, and upon arrest show no signs of remorse. Some may have no moral sense due to the harmful effects of drugs on the brain; others have learned only the moral standard of "might makes right." If there are no moral principles, then power rules. And if power rules, spiritual growth is impeded.

Is there a role for shame and guilt today? If we believe in right and wrong, then there is a role for shame. Shame rests on the adult judgment that there is something to be ashamed of.[1] This implies there are standards beyond my own personal opinion. If there are standards, they can and should be taught. Children can learn right from wrong, and they can be ashamed of wrongdoing.

In the popular mind, shame and guilt are attributes of conscience. We feel ashamed or guilty because we have done something wrong. This is highly appropriate. Yet we as a culture spend a fair amount of time trying to get rid of our "guilt feelings." This can be appropriate, for we can feel guilty for things beyond our responsibility. A friend of mine occasionally has attacks of guilt and anxiety over decisions, even correct ones, that he made long ago. He wonders if they were the best possible ones for the lives of those involved. He has guilt that is inappropriate. His emotions are separated from his common sense.

We also can and should feel guilty about our wrongdoing. Ethnic cleansing or assisted suicide should make us feel guilty! Serious wrongs need to be acknowledged and healed, not numbed through therapy or drugs.

We shape our consciences by our day-to-day decisions. What we decide to do or not to do helps to make us who we are. We form character by means of our deeds. Thus we see the importance of becoming more aware of the processes by which we have formed our own consciences and the steps we might take to achieve deeper moral awareness.

Conscience, at root, concerns our moral decision making. In an age in which people value autonomy, personal conscience rather than objective standards has come to the fore. Yet if anyone, from my next door neighbors to the Nazi doctors of World War II, can appeal to conscience to justify variant forms of activity, what can conscience mean?

The Meaning of Conscience

What is conscience? Sigmund Freud, the father of modern psychology, referred to the superego as conscience. In this I believe he was mistaken. In Freudian terms conscience is part of the superego.[2] It is the sum total of the prohibitions and rules we learn from our parents.

In Christian terms, conscience is part of the ego. We make our own decisions. Conscience invites us to action, is extroverted and dynamic, and oriented to true value. Conscience in Freudian terms pertains to the early stages of human development, when we were children. Conscience in Christianity pertains to responsible adulthood.[3]

The bishops at Vatican II said that conscience is the "secret core and...sanctuary"[4] of the person. It pertains to the deepest part of our humanity.

Conscience might most helpfully be considered to have

three levels.[5] At the deepest level, we have an awareness of "how it is with ourselves."[6] We have some sense of how we are doing and that our lives are in order. Deep down we know whether things are okay or not.

The second level is that of the more generalized awareness we have of right and wrong. At this level, we have an awareness of basic moral principles. This is built into our very humanity. We are rational creatures with certain basic inclinations or needs pointing us toward the goods that fulfill us. Here we have the basis for traditional Catholic thinking about natural law. God speaks to us through our human nature. We have in our hearts a law written by God.[7]

The third level of conscience is that of practical decision making or discernment. Here we choose "to do this" or "not to do that." We bring the moral principles of the second level to bear on a situation with sensitivity to the circumstances and the people involved. This calls for practical wisdom. We will discuss such moral discernments in more detail in the following chapter.

A Developing Natural law

Moral truth guides moral decision making. How are we to get to the truth? This is a very important contemporary question. Some hold that there is no truth, only opinion or feelings. Christians believe that there are moral truths that should form our conscientious decision making. Such truths come to us as individuals and as a community in the many ways God speaks to us. This includes the Scriptures and our own human nature, made in God's image.

Sacred Scripture and the church community present us with many fundamental principles that inform our decision making. Yet in traditional Catholic thinking, principles of conscience can also be deduced by our natural ability to reason.[8] These principles are available to all, not just to believers.

Systematic attention to our ability to come reasonably to moral principles is part of the classic consideration of natural law. Natural law has had many varied advocates over more than twenty centuries. It is not a monolithic system but a living school of thought.[9]

Contemporary natural-law thinking is quite dynamic. Contemporary natural-law thinkers believe that moral principles and the human inclinations, goods and goals that underlie these principles can always be understood better. The truth is capable of further analysis, better understanding and wiser application. Dialogue and discussion of principles and issues characterize this dynamic movement.

The benchmark of natural-law thought in the Catholic community is that of St. Thomas Aquinas. His brilliant synthesis of Greek philosophy (especially that of Aristotle) with Christianity set the standard for all who follow. Aquinas has many modern expositors who advocate varying and divergent interpretations of his thought. They maintain his central insights while engaging in their own dialogue with the modern world.[10]

Realist (sometimes called "common sense") philosophy grounds natural-law thinking; systematic thought is intrinsic to its identity. Thus, traditional natural-law thinkers, while upholding the absolute value of life, always seek to understand human dignity more fully. The evolution of thinking on capital punishment is one instance of this dynamic. More and more, these thinkers hold that capital punishment is contrary to respect for the dignity of the person and violates the dignity of the executioners as well.

Natural-law thinkers look systematically at the connection between moral cases. If principle A is admitted in this moral decision, then how will it affect our moral judgments about other cases? To my mind, a central example of the importance of systematic thinking is the Catholic controversy over artificial contraception. One significant point in this complex controversy is its implications. If we say that results are the critical factor in justifying artificial means of contraception, then shouldn't results also justify abortion, euthanasia, medical experimentation and so forth? The secular culture, driven by the pragmatism of results, already endorses many significant deviations from classical Christian moral thought. Natural-law thinkers question whether this endorsement serves human dignity at present and in the long run. And they believe it is contrary to the teaching of Scripture as well.

The foundations and arguments for natural law are too complex to be summarized here. St. Paul, in his letter to the Romans, contends that this law is written in our hearts and is accessible to conscience. Centuries of Christian thought have reflected on his basic insight and its implications.

The Formation of Conscience

As we have just noted in our discussion of natural law, the formation of our consciences is an ongoing process. We can always understand the truth and our human dignity more fully. There is always need for progress.

> The never-ending search which every man [sic] must undertake for himself in order to find out what is worthy of a man and what is not worthy of a man is what we call the "formation" of his conscience.[11]

We do not form our consciences in a vacuum. We belong to communities and to a nation. The confusion and tension in the church after the Second Vatican Council comprise the context in which we have, in fact, formed our consciences.

The moral permissiveness, the "everybody is doing it so it must be okay" mentality of contemporary American culture, also has had a profound influence on us.

We tend to react to the moral confusion around us in a variety of ways. One response is that of the static or complacent conscience. "Just tell me what to do and I'll do it" is the attitude of some. This throws all responsibility onto the church or some other decision maker. It short-circuits our own responsibility to grow spiritually.

Another attitude is the revolutionary conscience. "No one can tell me what to do." It is the attitude of personal infallibility mentioned earlier. All standards are those held by the individual. There is an element of truth in this attitude in that a well-formed conscience is the ultimate forum—we must follow our consciences. But the formation of conscience is far from an individual act alone.

We must continue to grow in the freedom in which we are to make balanced judgments and avoid the extremes just mentioned. As we will discuss more fully in the next chapter, we are not completely free. We have from our upbringing and our life experience certain areas of our lives where compulsion or ignorance rule. We often aren't aware of these blind spots. Once we become aware of them, however, our task is to become free from those patterns that cause us to think and act wrongly.

A related matter is our inner disability caused by past patterns of sin. For example, we may have learned to blaspheme profusely in the military. We still carry this sinful pattern with us.

> In relation to the moral situation and its demand, sin may be understood as the disabling factor that sometimes prevents the appropriate response to the demand; while grace is the enabling factor that sometimes permits the response to take place.[12]

One task in our formation of conscience is to work assiduously to regain our freedom, to gradually forsake our habit of blaspheming in favor of a loving response to God and others. Here we move from the blindness of sin to a deeper awareness. This is the result of our strenuous efforts with help from others. It is also the result of God's enabling work, the grace of the Holy Spirit.

Faith is another critical element in conscience formation. As we turn our lives more to God; as we accept Jesus as the Way, the Truth and the Life; as we live more in the Holy Spirit we grow in our conscientiousness. Our minds are formed more by the good news of the Gospel. We listen more sensitively to the variety of ways God speaks to us. We realize more fully that God calls us beyond the minimums of the law to holiness.

As we form our consciences more deeply, we become more human. We maximize the capabilities of our human nature. Part of this maximization is recognizing that progress in our understanding of the spiritual and moral life can be slow. This progress admits, however, of certain recognizable patterns.

Developmental Aspects of Moral Growth

The late psychologist Lawrence Kohlberg laid out in some detail the patterns of moral reasoning through which individuals progress as they grow to maturity. Individuals develop from preconventional to conventional to post-conventional ways of reasoning about moral dilemmas.

In short, for the preconventional moral reasoner what is good for the individual is good; for the conventional person what is good for society is good; for the postconventional person what is good for any human person is good.[13]

This progress is a lifelong process. We grow in our ability to reason more effectively in interaction with others who challenge our ways of thinking. Kohlberg argues that our actions usually—I would say often—follow our ways of thinking about moral questions.

While Kohlberg's theory of development has generated much criticism,[14] it also seems to have some basic validity. People do go through stages in their progression toward better moral reasoning. His first two levels seem to be basically accurate in their depictions. For our purposes, it is significant to note that progress in moral reasoning can be a lifetime process that goes on with the help of others.

A challenge to Kohlberg's work came in the 1980s from his colleague, Carol Gilligan. She argued for the importance of relationships in the moral development of women. Women tend to respond to moral dilemmas in terms of the relationships involved. For instance, how will this decision affect the relationships of the other people in the moral situation? The importance of relationships was somewhat lost in Kohlberg's stress on growing autonomy in rational moral decision making. Recent studies indicate some differences in men and women in assessing moral dilemmas but show that both men and women can look to moral principles and relationships in making moral judgments.[15]

Thus we see affirmed from another angle the importance of relationships in moral growth. This also alerts us to the fact that friends and acquaintances might emphasize different principles and relationships in coming to their conscientious conclusions.

The critic Christopher Lasch cautions us that we should not overemphasize relationships too much. He believes the both Kohlberg and Gilligan err in not understanding

...that the only escape from the polarity of egoism and altruism lies in the selflessness experienced by those who lose themselves in their work, in the effort to master a craft or a body of knowledge, or in the acceptance of a formidable challenge that calls on all their resources. It is only in purposeful activity that we find a suspension of egoism that goes beyond conventional self-sacrifice.[16]

Lasch believes that Gilligan's study of adolescent girls shows that relationships can be destructive as well as constructive. "...[W]omen are just as likely as men to misuse power, to relish cruelty, and to indulge the taste for cruelty in enforcing conformity."[17]

Practical Moral Growth

Lasch's good sense in pointing out the pitfalls of our focus on relationships is sobering. It reminds us that relationships can make for ill as well as for good—for vice as well as for virtue. For example, narrow group or ethnic thinking can lead to policies of discrimination or death such as we have seen in recent bouts of ethnic and tribal strife around the world.

In this context, we now turn to the personal encounters and events that can influence the positive development of our consciences. "These events are called here (a) marker events, (b) relational commitments and (c) religious experiences."[18]

Marker events such as marriage, death, divorce, trauma or unexpected success can have great effects on us. These events may come because of our choices. They also may be the results of events out of our control, such as an economic downturn or a business restructuring. They can help or even impel us to look at ourselves anew or to think differently about ourselves. They can cause people to regard us in a different way.

Friends of mine recently retired and moved to the mountains. They built a brand new home with a magnificent view.

There is plenty of room for friends and family to come to visit. This positive experience is a challenge as well. Living in a small town is different than living in a major metropolitan area. There are new friends to make. Old patterns are reexamined as one sorts the accumulated possessions of thirty years to determine what to keep. New patterns can emerge in marital communication or in faith—as well as in where to put the toothpaste or store the grandchildren's toys.

Such marker events drive us to look at our principles from a new angle and affirm once again the relationships and communities that give us life. They invite us to go deeper in our understanding and commitment.

Commitments to new relationships likewise can change us and influence our conscientious judgments. New colleagues and companions can raise our self-esteem or dash it. They call forth new or latent talents. They can lead us to be sensitive to others in different ways. Those in leadership can be challenged to integrate the talents of new colleagues with those of people already at work, thus maximizing the contributions and effectiveness of all.

A third aspect of moral growth is religious conversion. At times we meet God more directly. This is usually not so dramatic as St. Paul being knocked off his horse or St. Augustine hearing a voice in the garden telling him to "take up and read" the Scriptures. But it is real.

Conversion here can mean that the disparate parts of our lives have come together. It can mean a change of direction. It can mean yielding our lives to God and letting go of the control we thought we had. Conversion can be dramatic, as it was for my friend whose near-death on his daily motorcycle ride led him to reconsider his life's direction.

For most of us conversion is by accumulation. We gradually get to the point where we choose to change. This may be because of certain marker events and relationships as well as personal encounters with God. In practice these existential elements often mix together.

Formation in Community

The formation of conscience involves our coming to grasp the moral principles of natural law and Scripture (as best we are able) as well as our integrating the events and relationships of our lives. This formation is affected by our level of emotional and intellectual maturity as well as by our cultural and social background. My handicapped cousin has less capability than most people for sophisticated levels of moral understanding. Yet he can make some good moral decisions based on what he has learned in his family life.

Formation of conscience is a complex reality, and there are a variety of paths to good decision making. We form our consciences within the Christian community. Here we encounter the Scriptures, Tradition, prayer life, sacraments, laws and personal challenges that can make for a positive formation. Our conscience is not always correct; we are bound to follow it but it may err. In the community we have others to ask about our decisions of conscience: Do I seem to be on the right track? How can I do better?

A major question arises when we consult the community—whether individual members or those in official positions—and we don't agree with them. If we differ with some individuals, we might consult others before making our judgments, or we might seek out the position of the church on the particular issue—if there is one.

A more common issue today concerns conscientious personal decisions contrary to the teachings of the community. These are sometimes referred to as questions of dissent.[19] If we consult those who hold official positions and enunciate the position of the church community, can we continue to act on our own conscientiously held positions? This issue is widely discussed in those Christian communities where commitment is to a creed, to a corpus of doctrine. We begin here by noting with Macquarrie that

> Only when he [sic] has endeavored to the utmost of his ability, to make allowance for his own tendencies toward distortion and egocentricity can a person justifiably set up his own conscience in opposition to the commonly accepted code.[20]

Only when a person has fully entered into dialogue with the community and come to understand its stance thoroughly is there a possibility of withholding one's consent. "Scripture, worship, prayer, the witness and counsel of fellow Christians, and the teaching authority of the church all inform one's inner dialogue."[21]

Catholic Christians in particular inform their consciences by turning to the church and its multiple forms of authority. The presumption is that the church is right on a particular issue. A "lack of assent" is possible—the innovative ideas of Yves Congar and John Courtney Murray led to change in the church at Vatican II. Their work later led to constructive transformation. Other stands do not. A parish in Louisiana had to be disciplined in the early 1960s for its stand against the church's teaching on racial justice. Dissent may be for good or ill; often we know the results in hindsight.

One interesting fact is that those whose differing views eventually led to effective change at Vatican II were willing to submit, with suffering to be sure, to church discipline. Their spiritual attitude led to moral success. In coming to our own conscientious decisions, which we are ultimately bound to follow, we must consider the whole question of our ability to deal with disappointment and even suffering.

No matter what our age, we learn to act conscientiously by the example of conscientious members of the community. "The wise" who make good moral judgments are available to us to help in our conscientious decision making. We are only alone if we choose to be.

We are complex creatures, and we can use the help of others in forming our consciences. This formation goes on throughout life.

> The real world of moral choices depends more upon our character, our habits, vision, affections and countless other nonrational factors than it does upon impersonal rules, rational abstractions and logical procedures. "What sort of person ought I to become?" or being a moral person is prior to the question "What should I do?"[22]

The saints in particular hold up to us an outstanding witness of what it means to be a follower of Christ. Such models of conscientious judgment help us in our own decision making. Our decisions in conscience move us to sanctity.

QUESTIONS FOR REFLECTION AND DISCUSSION

1. What are the factors that have most influenced the formation of your conscience up to this point in your life?

2. What is your response to authority in general and to church authority in particular?

VI. Moral Discernment

Educated at one of the country's top law schools, Steve had worked in the district attorney's office for several years. The hours had been long and the work sometimes tedious, but Steve had done well, winning his share of convictions. And, of course, there was the satisfaction of getting drug pushers off the streets and behind bars—on a good day Steve felt he was making a real contribution to society.

As he approached age forty, however, Steve began to have doubts about his chosen profession. Did he really want to stay in the legal field for the rest of his life? Corporate law did not appeal to him despite the lure of big money. And he was rapidly losing his taste for government bureaucracy. What he really wanted to do, he confided to a friend, was return to school and earn a degree in medicine. But could he afford—financially and in other ways—to give up a secure job, ask his wife to support him for several years, and venture into a brand new career?

Personal freedom is at the root of the formation of conscience. This freedom structures our moral decisions and determines the course of our lives. We move conscientiously toward making the best practical decisions regarding what we are to do here and now. This is sometimes referred to as the matter of discernment. What does God want me to do? How does this particular decision fit in with the overall pattern and goals of my life? How do I grow spiritually through this judgment?

Discernment concerns itself with making wise decisions

about courses of action. For instance, a person may have to make a decision about which career or job to pursue—a choice between two good things, as in the example above. Or it may be a matter of choosing between good and evil.

Our hope in this chapter is that reflection on the discernment process may help us to make better moral decisions. Good moral decision making can lead to peace of mind. We are able to "live with ourselves," as the saying goes. But we need to know exactly what goes into this wise decision making.

We may begin by asking ourselves how we really make our day-to-day decisions. Often we like to appear quite rational, and, as a result, we may offer some overtly "acceptable" reasons for the decisions we make. Yet at times there is a difference between good reasons and the real reason. We sometimes offer a reason that is publicly acceptable rather than reveal our true interests and concerns.

Often, our decisions arise from how we feel. Our emotions dominate. We decide based on the mood of the moment. If we are honest with ourselves, we may have to admit that this is our dominant way of deciding. And we might question whether emotion should dominate in daily decision making.

At other times, we may be typically American, making our decisions based on results. If it works, it is okay. Practical results are what counts. While this pragmatic attitude might be good for engineers—"If it is an inch short, it's not a bridge"—it may not always be morally wise.

Purely pragmatic decisions leave no room for human dignity. They reduce the human to the functional. Thus the person who is handicapped—not optimally functional by reason of birth, accident or age—serves no pragmatic value and can be discarded.

Recently my Aunt Margaret died at ninety-six. She had

lived a long life and departed quietly and gently, just as she had lived. In her last several years, Aunt Margaret didn't know any of our family. Her memory was completely gone. Previously, she knew that she didn't know. At the end, she didn't know that either. In pragmatic terms, Aunt Margaret's long life had turned useless. Her residence in the nursing home was expensive, and she served no utilitarian purpose. Yet her basic goodness and human dignity were obviously with her to the end. We grew by visiting her. And God was and is glorified in her very being.

The critical question here is of human worth and intrinsic value. Catholics and many other Christians have always held, basing themselves on Scripture and natural law, that issues of human good and principles of morality transcend the mood of the moment and pragmatic calculations. Aunt Margaret's life was good, even if not optimally functional.

Classically, we as a community have advocated an objective morality. That is, we argue that there are moral principles based in reality, in the truth of human nature and divine revelation, that should not be violated.

These principles, such as the dignity of human life, can always be comprehended more fully and practiced more effectively. They need to be applied to individual situations with a loving wisdom that takes into account the varieties of circumstances and relationships. At times they still leave us with the rigors of practical decision making. Yet they provide the guidance that points to what we should or should not do.

The role of such *shoulds* is vital to a moral life. At times, the vision of our goal or our best impulses fail to motivate us—we couldn't care less about anything. Yet we know that we should do the right thing. We should help our brother with his move to a new home even if we don't feel like it.

We should visit a sick friend in the hospital, but hospitals make us uncomfortable. These are the right things to do even though at the moment we'd rather be somewhere else. Keeping the *shoulds* is a sign of coming to spiritual maturity. We do what is right, we keep our commitments and are not dominated by the mood of the moment.

Criteria for Moral Decisions

In making our moral decisions for the good, we have some classical points of reflection to help us. First of all, we need to look at what we are doing. What kind of act are we thinking about? How does this particular action measure up to the moral standards upheld by the Ten Commandments, the Beatitudes (Mt 5:1–12) or the natural law?[1] Will this type of action lead us to God?

Traditionally, the Catholic community has believed that certain types of action, technically called intrinsically evil, will never be in accord with God's will. They will never lead us to our heavenly home. They do not make for holiness or human fulfillment. Violations of human life such as abortion, euthanasia or murder fall into this category. So too do sexual violations such as rape, incest, adultery or fornication. No circumstances or consequences would justify such acts.

Yet in many other acts, circumstances and consequences bear heavily on our decisions. These add a further moral dimension to our decision making. The *who, where, when* and *with what* of our decisions add a distinct coloration to most of these decisions and affect many of our choices. The circumstances of Aunt Margaret's last days led the family to decide against extraordinary means such as a "code blue," while still maintaining the nutrition and comfort care that respected the intrinsic dignity of her life.

If an act and its circumstances form the objective structure of the classical analysis of human conduct, then our intentions or motives—the subjective side of our acting—are perhaps of greater contemporary interest. Having anchored our communal morality in reality, in the truth, in contrast to current normlessness, we come to consider ourselves. How responsible are we?

The truth is that we are very responsible. When we know what we are doing and choose to do it, we can justifiably take pride in our good actions and be ashamed of our evil ones.

Our choice of evil is real and is our responsibility. We *do* sin, even though we hate to admit it and seek to rationalize our choices away. Several colleagues of mine who have worked in the prison ministry report that among long-term prisoners, they found not one who considered him- or herself guilty. All were "innocent" and "mistakenly" imprisoned. Such is the power of rationalization or denial.

Denial of responsibility is not just for prisoners; it is publicly visible all around us. Rather than acknowledging standards and admitting when we fail, it sometimes seems that we see responsibility more as a public relations or "spin" problem. To my mind, this situation reflects the valueless nature of public discourse. If there are no real moral standards, but only laws reflecting the changing will of the majority, then why take responsibility? Personal integrity comes in living by a moral code. If there is no code, then it is best to follow the opinion polls.

Yet, even if we are struggling to take responsibility and live by moral principle, we can still have our doubts. How much I knew and how clearly I was aware of my choice of a good or evil act may be cloudy in my mind—especially if some time has elapsed since the act in question.

Besides denial, cloudiness of memory and midlife memory lapses, there are also other impediments that influence our judgments. The power of habit may lead to a thought-less act stemming from a previous pattern of acting that we have abandoned long ago or are attempting to change now. Ignorance may keep us from making good choices due to no fault of our own. External forces or internal fears may impede us from doing the good or avoiding the evil that our best selves see as moral and necessary.

In particular, we might note that in his encyclical on life, *Evangelium Vitae,* John Paul II opposes "crimes against life." Yet for individual persons, the Pope understands that:

> Decisions that go against life sometimes arise from difficult or even tragic situations of profound suffering, loneliness, a total lack of economic prospects, depression and anxiety about the future. Such circumstances can mitigate even to a notable degree subjective responsibility and the consequent culpability of those who make these choices. (No. 18)

Further, he readily grants that decisions for abortion, though morally unjustifiable, are often "not made for purely selfish reasons or out of convenience, but out of a desire to protect certain important values such as [the woman's] own health or a decent standard of living for the other members of the family" (No. 58).[2]

There are numerous factors that can influence personal responsibility for good or evil actions. While our presumption is that we are the authors of our deeds, mitigating factors of upbringing and circumstance can seriously impede our acting with full freedom and understanding.

Of particular interest these days is the question of addiction. How responsible are we for our actions if we suffer from the disease of alcoholism, drug addiction or some other compulsion? Certain patterns of action may be deeply rooted in a dysfunctional upbringing. We may not really be free in these areas.

In these situations our basic human freedom remains.

With the help of others and of God, we can choose to attain and maintain recovery. This certainly is the work of grace. But it is also the work of the individual. After we recognize our "unfreedom" and dysfunction, our obligation is to become free. In those areas of our lives where we act compulsively, we must work to regain our freedom. This process of regaining our freedom may be lengthy. One priest who counsels alcoholics told me that he believes that it can take five years to regain freedom and responsibility.

Many of us, on looking at our lives, realize that we have areas where sinful patterns of action dominate. We have areas of unfreedom, though not to such a pervasive extent as those who suffer from addictions. Our responsibility is to regain our freedom with God's help. And it is also our responsibility to acknowledge that in most of our decisions we are truly free. Even those seriously addicted have significant parts of their lives where freedom dominates and is to be claimed.

Discerning the Good

In freedom, we make decisions. Mostly these decisions are minor; at times, they are more significant. They may not involve choosing between good or evil, but rather choosing between good paths. Should I pursue one career or another, like Steve whom we mentioned earlier? Should I go back to school or continue working? Should I visit the sick or teach religious education?

These questions call us to listen to God's call most intently. They call for wise decision making. The Christian spiritual tradition, drawing on the teachings of the saints, provides us with some guidance in these matters of choosing between good courses of action.

Discernment is well attested to in the New Testament and in the Catholic Tradition.[3] St. Francis de Sales, in his varied works, lists a number of criteria for discernment.[4] These criteria should be used within a context of prayer and reflection, as with all moral decision making. Discernment here, it should be noted, is not an exact process, like solving an equation in mathematics. Rather, it involves wise decision making, using the best internal and external criteria. Some of these criteria are noted in de Sales's works:

1. GOD'S SIGNIFIED WILL—God has already taught us many things through the commandments, counsels, inspirations, natural law and so forth. These provide parameters within which we make our discernments.

2. THE COMMUNAL PROCESS—As Christians, we are part of a community. Our gifts are to be shared. Our best judgments, especially in important matters, are made with the help of our wise spiritual friends. They will often see things we don't see about ourselves or about the situation that are invaluable in helping us to discern.

3. FREEDOM OF SPIRIT—Each person is unique. Each is moved by the Holy Spirit in a particular way. Each has gifts to give. Thus discernment will not be exactly the same for each person. Furthermore, a certain flexibility is necessary. God may call us for a time beyond our customary way of doing things to something new. Or we may be asked to leave our habitual ways for a work(s) of charity. God can and does call us beyond ourselves.

4. PERSEVERANCE IN OUR VOCATION—While flexibility is necessary, perseverance in one's vocation or present duty is essential for spiritual growth. De Sales's presumption is against change in one's vocation. Today, American society is more mobile than those of former times, but the question of commitment and perseverance is still crucial.

5. AFFECTIVE STATES—The presence of certain interior affective states can also indicate the movement of the Spirit.

a. JOY—For de Sales, holiness is appealing and happy. The awareness of God's constant love "cannot be without an inner joy even in the midst of difficulties."[5]

b. PEACE OR TRANQUILITY—The movement of the Holy Spirit is gentle, sweet and peaceful. A freedom from anxiety and a deep inner peacefulness is an authentic sign of the Spirit.

c. CONSOLATION/DESOLATION—Sensible satisfaction in prayer or the absence thereof is a more difficult criterion to use. Consolation in prayer can be deceiving and should be examined in light of the fruitfulness of that prayer in good works. Desolation or dryness in prayer may indicate that discernment is on the wrong track, but it might originate in personal fault or resistance to God. Or it may even be a call to greater spiritual depth. Thus these inner states must not be given excessive weight, but must be seen in the light of the other criteria.

6. VIRTUES—Good discernment flows from and leads to a greater depth in virtue. Three virtues are manifest in particular.

a. HUMILITY—With this virtue, we see ourselves as we truly are—neither denying our real gifts nor our complete dependence on God. Humility is realism about who we are before God. While getting to know ourselves is the work of a lifetime, such realism is crucial to good discernment.

b. OBEDIENCE—While often downplayed in demo-
cratic and individualistic societies, obedience to legit-
imate authority is significant to true discernment.
Obedience in Salesian thought can be conceived
widely[6] but at its root it is a safeguard against egoism
and a tendency to over- or undervalue one's talents.

c. CHARITY—This central virtue culminates the
process of discernment. Growth in charity is the
sine qua non of discernment. The demands of charity are the final test of discernment of God's will.
True love expresses itself in action.

Authority in the Holy Spirit

Discernment, moral decision making, and growth in
virtue are not only the work of reason and analysis; they are
even more the work of the Holy Spirit in our lives. Christians receive the Spirit in Baptism. They live the life of the
Spirit, however imperfectly. They seek the guidance of the
Spirit in decision making.

The Spirit is in the church as a whole, not just in those
who have the gift of leadership and authority. We need to
learn from one another for proper discernment. We need to
listen to authorities in order to make good decisions. And
we also need to accept our particular personal areas of
responsibility in the community.

Authority in the church is a multifaceted reality. If we are
in the Spirit, then we have to take the lead—in giving good
example by our lives of prayer and good works; in fulfilling
family responsibilities; in meeting new challenges as they
arise; and in accepting positions of responsibility (and
stress) when the Spirit calls.

Authority certainly rests in the inspired word of Scripture, which we discussed in our second chapter. Our discernments and decisions at their best arise from a mind formed by God's word and captivated by the strength and truth of biblical teachings. The Spirit continues to guide us through the word of personal inspiration and public proclamation.

The Spirit also speaks to us through Tradition. This is the Tradition with a capital *T*, not the small *t* traditions of customs such as celebrating sacraments in Latin or Old English or rehearsing certain prayers and rites. This Tradition includes the Scriptures, expresses itself preeminently in ecumenical councils, and is the continuing and definitive work of the Spirit in history. God has continued to speak to us and, at times, in ways that are binding for the whole community.

We need to grapple with this Tradition and let it form us. Thus we see the importance of the *Catechism of the Catholic Church*[7] as the most recent (and always inadequate) attempt to capture the work of the Spirit in history. We can and should spend a lifetime seeking to penetrate the continuing work of the Spirit and let it penetrate us. Our need to embrace Tradition has perhaps been underestimated in this era of church history in which the focus has been on the inspired word of the Bible. Yet we are called to listen to God in the variety of ways he addresses us. The inspired Tradition needs likewise to be part of our prayer and insight.

As if Scripture and Tradition were not enough to keep us busy for a lifetime, God raises up from time to time prophetic individuals in the community to call us to the fundamentals and to the highest standards. St. Francis of Assisi, with his simplicity, his emphasis on poverty and his lyric mysticism is one such person.

Our practical, present-day difficulty lies in distinguishing the true from the false prophets. Prophets can be a bit eccentric by conventional standards. Our local communities always tend to attract a few eccentrics who might even wish to be prophets but are just eccentric. True prophetic individuals can also make us uncomfortable by questioning our compromises and challenging us to higher standards. All this makes judging the true from the false prophet quite difficult in practice. Yet we know we need to continue to be open to such individuals sent by God if we are to live the gospel faithfully.

If deciphering true prophets in our midst is difficult, so too is discerning the sense of the faithful. We are a community that shares a faith, and we have a sense of what it is. Yet all of us are not living equally in the Spirit of Christ, and thus all are not equally in touch with the faith. In fact, we have a number of believers whose yearly appearances in church are limited to the great feasts of Christmas and Easter. Others even limit themselves to coming only to be "hatched, matched and dispatched." Our communities tend to diversity, and it is rare that someone is excommunicated. Thus we will always have an admixture of saints and sinners, the devout and the tepid.

Grasping the sense of the faithful will always be a challenge. No mere opinion poll will do; discernment here will involve listening to arguments pro and con as well as observing the faithfully lived lives of believers. I believe that one recent instance in the Catholic community of sensitivity to the demands of the faith is the pro-life movement. This movement arose among the Catholic laity in defense of a basic moral principle.

Another authoritative group within the community is theologians. These professionally trained scholars of the faith have held a prominent role throughout Christian history in helping us to understand and interpret the faith. Their training provides us with a useful tool to aid in the discernment processes just mentioned. They seek to penetrate the truths of faith more profoundly, to understand them more fully and to share them more widely than heretofore accomplished. They seek to make the faith available to people in a contemporary and accessible language. Theologians are women and men of their time and are subject to all the secular currents around us. Thus they need a strong life of prayer. In addition, they need to dialogue with fellow theologians and with the bishops in order to purge personal idiosyncrasies as they pursue the truths of faith and the good of the community of faith.

The holders of authoritative positions in the community—the pope and bishops—have special authority and special responsibilities. Their discernments in dialogue with the community can be definitive, as stated at the Second Vatican Council.[8] Their roles are difficult ones in a community as large as the Catholic Church. The role of the papacy in particular, as the world's most visible religious position, calls for extraordinary balance and sensitivity.

All sizable Christian denominations are structured. For some this may be a bit more implicit than explicit—but no large organization today can escape a certain routinization and bureaucratization of function. The Roman Curia is the most obvious example of this. Tension arises for us as well as for those of other Christian communities as the American penchant for democracy runs into the hierarchical structures of Catholicism. We Americans yearn for some "checks and balances" of authority, especially when we find that authority a little too challenging or thwarting. The Tradition argues for the Spirit-inspired hierarchical nature of the community as a safeguard for the continuity of faith.

Authorities are to teach the faith of the church. The pope and bishops are servants of the faith and not its arbitrary interpreters. So too are pastors and lay ministers. The Holy Spirit guides the church to a deeper understanding of faith; this is an ongoing process. Nowadays important documents, such as the new catechism, are the fruit of prolonged consultation. This helps assure their faithfulness to the Scripture and Tradition upon which the community bases itself.[9]

Our discussion of the various authorities in the church community that affect our moral decision making might conclude with the observation that most authority is local. The invisible day-to-day decisions are the most frequent. Authority is exercised by educators, parents and pastoral ministers as well as by pastors. Authority often flows as much from example as from words. Our service is visible, not merely verbal. Mother Teresa led mostly by her integrity and witness of care for the poor. All of us are called to exercise our particular authority in the community and to make sensitive moral discernments for the good of all.

QUESTIONS FOR REFLECTION AND DISCUSSION

1. How do you really go about making your moral decisions? How influential are your emotions in this process?

2. At present, what is your process of discernment? In light of our discussion, might you modify this process?

3. How do you view authority, both civil and religious? What role does authority play in your moral discernment and decision making?

VII. Working in Faith So That All May Be One

*W*e cannot escape the reality that the Christian community today is divided. As we have discussed, Catholicism and other Christian denominations are experiencing various divisions and the rise of opposing groups within their communities. The reality of conflict and disagreement is readily apparent. We see protests of various types for different causes—some related to the issues of authority that we mentioned in the preceding chapter.

Occasionally, at the Sunday eucharist in a local parish, I see a man who stands during the eucharistic prayer while everyone else kneels. I suppose he is conducting a protest of some type, but I don't know what his cause is since there are so many these days. Since he always leaves the mass early, I may never know what he is "standing up for."

A recent attempt to acknowledge and address some of the issues dividing our community today is the Common Ground Project. The late Cardinal Bernardin sought to bring together some of the disparate groups in the Catholic Church to speak with one another. The Cardinal's colleagues are continuing this project.

This project has generated quite a bit of discussion— some heat and some light.[1] Many outstanding church leaders have taken differing positions in this ongoing discussion. Such discussions are needed if healing is to take place and if we are to grow in our ability to follow the Holy

Spirit in forming our consciences and making good moral decisions. Our purpose in this chapter, however, is more modest. We will not be discussing reconciliation as it applies to national issues affecting the church. Our focus will be on local conditions. Doctrine is not our primary concern, but rather the local community where our day-to-day growth in holiness is taking place.

We should not think of healing as solely personal or interpersonal.[2] We need healing in our local parishes and civil communities as well as in our relationships with God and neighbor. These communities support our relational lives and form the context of our living. Without vibrant communities, our spiritual and moral lives wither. They help us to become virtuous, good-living people. Thus, we will turn briefly to healing processes in these communities.

The Christian community itself seeks to be a healing community in the work that it does for the poor and those in need. The works of mercy are most characteristic of Christianity and are evident in our local parish communities and dioceses as well as in national groups such as Catholic Charities. We as a community seek to be a reconciling, compassionate presence to those in need whether they be the homeless or the aged. I think, for example, of Project Rachel. This is the church's healing effort to help women who have had abortions and, later in life, experience stress and personal difficulties in coming to terms with their choices.

As a healing community, we also need to pray that *we* be healed. We need to ask for forgiveness for any evil that has been done in our name. Some former members are no longer in our midst because we as a group did not show the concern and love of Christ. Humility, not hubris, should be our proper stance.

At times, too, scandal has wounded the parish community

itself. I think of the recent spate of cases of priests who have committed pedophilia. Here we need, from both leaders and parishioners, a healing response for all concerned.

Leadership is an urgent necessity in parishes that have experienced such cases of sexual abuse. There is a need for healing here. The church leaders, in particular the bishop, must take responsibility before the community. There are times when a parish needs to hear directly from its spiritual leader. One of those times is when allegations of clergy-child sexual abuse are made:

> Some bishops have made announcements from the parish pulpit. Others have offered a mass of healing in the parish. Still others have sent personal messages via an episcopal vicar.
>
> In the early stages, the bishop may have few answers. However, his authoritative presence communicates the most important message: he is concerned with the parishioners' pain and wants to help.[3]

Conflict—Part of the Human Condition

If compassion and healing are what we are about in our Christian communities, we also recognize that in our lives we are never free of disagreement, division and conflict. It happens internally as we struggle to live more perfectly. Like St. Paul, we do not do the good we will, and we do the evil we do not wish. Conflict occurs in our interpersonal relationships within our families, our communities, at our jobs and in our parishes. It happens between groups who hold different perspectives within our organizations, our churches and our governments. It happens between nations.

When disagreement or division occurs within the fold of the church, it can be particularly troublesome. Christ's prayer was that "they all may be one, as you Father are in Me, and I in you; that they may be one in us" (Jn 17:21). Dispute and conflict within the church, if not addressed and resolved, interfere with the ability of individual members to grow spiritually, and can shatter the unity of the people of God, for which Christ prayed so fervently. We have an obligation as Christians to seek resolutions to conflicts within the church since such situations have divisive and destructive repercussions.

There is a tendency of groups in the church to adopt the "political party" model of church, and the desire to win is part of this frame of reference. Whether this model is appropriate to the church is questionable. We need to look at the relationship between our personal views toward the teachings of Christ and those of the Catholic Tradition and seriously question our grasp of the whole, rather than simply excommunicating those who differ from our group. Christ calls the church to be a reconciling community, and thus we need to work together in a charitable and loving way.

This call to work together, to be one, is particularly poignant as we enter more and more into the era of collaborative ministry. If we are to work together, we need ways to resolve some of our differences. In the fractious contemporary church, we will need to learn to handle criticism. Those of us who are hyper sensitive will have to learn to cope—for division is here to stay. Nowadays we seem to be more the fractious church of the Middle Ages than the more uniform church of the last century.

In this context, we have to ask ourselves how we respond to criticism even if it might be justified.[4] Some of us get angry; some of us withdraw; and others become aggressive or perfectionistic.

Better ways to respond might include stopping for a

minute to analyze the situation, to notice our personal dis-
tortions, and to seek more effective approaches than our
accustomed patterns. In this process, we need to acknowledge valid criticisms. We are not infallible. We may also
need to look for some element of agreement in order to
deflect another's anger and begin a more constructive
period of dialogue.

Often we may not be sure what the underlying issue is
that provokes the criticism. We may need to gently probe to
see what is really at stake. We may have to probe at the
right time, overcoming our need to "get everything out in
the open" right away. Timing may be crucial for problem
solving.

The move to alternative solutions may include brain-
storming and negotiation. Or there may be some need for
mediation.

> ...conflict is usually difficult, often messy and frequently
> painful. Conflict which is confronted and managed or
> resolved leads to group cohesion. There are two important
> points underlying this belief. First, conflict has been con-
> fronted and not avoided. Second, as a result of the
> encounter, something positive (conflict management or res-
> olution) has happened. Only when these two conditions
> have been met can the group achieve cohesiveness. Until
> this occurs, the group is loosely-related individuals who
> lack any real binding relationships. There is no community
> and no collaboration.[5]

Collaboration is only possible if we can resolve conflict.
This takes a commitment of time and energy.

> When conflict erupts, the person's automatic response is to
> preserve his or her sense of self-esteem. This triggers a
> defensive reaction which interferes with the ability to listen
> clearly, think logically and act compassionately, all of which
> are prerequisites for effective conflict management.[6]

In dealing with conflict one needs to:

1. Acknowledge the presence of the conflict.
2. Define the cause.
3. Make decisions.
4. Defuse the emotion.[7]

Personality differences, which are commonly labeled as the source of conflict, are rarely if ever its real cause. People are capable of working well with many differing personalities, and differences only become an issue when one person's self-esteem is threatened by another.[8]

Sometimes our disagreements are so strong and so emotional that more than ordinary means of coming to agreement and dealing with differences need to be tried. One approach might come to the fore in this new era of groups in the church is mediation. These days, some church disputes are making their way into the civil courts. Such situations may make us wonder if the Gospel steps for reconciliation with our brothers and sisters have been followed.

If we reflect on the very nature of dispute, we see that sometimes disagreements are primarily intellectual or reflect different perspectives; in such cases we may be able to "agree to disagree." Disagreements handled this way do not interfere with our ability to live our spiritual lives. At other times, disagreement may involve our feelings and emotions, or may otherwise impact on our lives in strongly negative ways. Our ability to live fully and happily, and to pursue our own growth and development may be much impaired by such a dispute. Some conflicts so interfere with our thought processes and actions that they boil over into active efforts to attack or defend, and open hostility can result. When disputes so interfere with life processes that the parties' actions go beyond the bounds society has set and interfere unlawfully with the rights of others to live as they wish, then society has an ultimate (albeit often ineffective) dispute resolution system—the criminal justice system.

The modern court system, however, is a flawed vehicle for solving problems and resolving conflicts. In trials before a judge or a jury, one party "wins" and the other "loses." It is usually an all or nothing proposition, and it often leaves the parties unsatisfied. Even those who "win" a lawsuit often come out of the process emotionally exhausted and financially drained by a process that is combative and divisive. There is rarely any healing happening in a courthouse or in the court process. A legal case often takes years to be resolved, and the spiritual effect of a lawsuit on the parties can be deadly.

Few, if any, disputes among real people who are involved in any sort of ongoing relationship, are handled well in the court forum. The "I win-you lose" approach is psychologically destructive, and renders it difficult, if not impossible, for the parties to continue any sort of ongoing relationship. In recognition of this, and as a concession to the prohibitive cost of civil litigation, alternative means of resolving disputes have been evolving over the past twenty-five years. One of these is a new and fundamentally different dispute resolution model which has been implemented as an augmentation of (or as an alternative to) traditional trials by many of the civil courts in this country. It has great promise for our church as well. It is called mediation.

Mediation: A Better Way to Resolve Problems

In mediation, the parties do not argue their case to a third party (judge or jury), who then decides which party wins. Rather, they employ a third party (a mediator—a neutral party) as a moderator or facilitator to assist them in reaching a resolution of the conflict themselves. The mediator is not a judge and does not "decide" the matter. The mediator rather assists the parties to communicate more effectively, and to examine together the issues that separate them. The mediator helps the parties to recognize that the positions they take may not be (and usually are not) identical with what is really of concern—their interests. The mediator assists the parties to focus on their ongoing relationship, and thereafter to work out with each other a mutually acceptable accommodation.

Mediation has been used in the civil arena in solving problems great and small. It is valuable in resolving intrafamilial disputes, and while it may not necessarily restore love, it helps the parties involved to come to some sort of agreement as to how they will interact in the future. With the structure of an agreement in place, a degree of harmony is restored, which then allows for the redevelopment of deeper relationships. Marriages have been saved and relations between parents and their children have been made tolerable—even love has been restored—using mediation. The process is equally valuable in resolving multiparty issues of the utmost complexity and has been used to resolve very emotional, community wide disputes, such as the siting of a new jail, halfway house or interstate highway.

Conflict in the Church

The church today is filled with a panoply of disagreements and conflicts. While the doctrinal disputes tend to get the publicity, the majority of conflicts are less doctrinal and more personal. We will concern ourselves with these.

The effect of our disparate views is felt down to the smallest parish, where disagreements certainly exist, even if sometimes unstated. Note, for example, issues as diverse as the location of the tabernacle in church or the role of sex education in the parochial school/religious education program. The polarization and the vigor of the rhetoric employed have ramifications that are not merely academic, but pastoral as well.

Other issues sparking dissension and conflict exist in every diocese and in every parish. Some are momentous issues; others are so localized as to be peculiar to a given parish. An underlying issue in many parishes concerns the proper role of the priest and the status and function of the faithful. In other parishes, whether there is to be a parish advisory board or not, and whether it is to have any real influence or power are questions that lead to confrontations. The times of Sunday or daily masses or the availability of devotional services can often have significant impact and create friction among parishioners. As the "mystery" of the eucharistic sacrifice has been seemingly reduced, some parishioners long for a return to a Latin mass, while others vigorously oppose this "turning away from Vatican II."

Many Catholics yearn for more than they are currently offered or can even request (much less have the temerity to demand) in their local churches. Many have deep fears for the future of our church, for the future of their children as Catholic Christians and for the very many persons who are simply not reached in the first place. Against these more universal concerns, one can contrast the very real but purely local disputes, for example: what to do about the cantor at the 9:00 mass who sings so poorly that he detracts from the service, but since he has been doing it for twenty years, no one is willing to ask him to step down.

While certainly not a panacea, mediation could be an effective tool in resolving some underlying issues and disputes. In the disputes peculiar to a specific parish, there are a variety of "parties" who espouse various "positions." Usually these positions reflect cultural, religious or other underlying backgrounds (or biases). These positions, as noted above, may have little relation to what is really important to them—their "interests."

Fundamentally we Catholics are all one, and it was Christ's prayer that we be one. We can only be one— become one—when we learn to focus on what is in our best interest, and to distinguish that from the positions we all too frequently take and defend against our brothers and sisters, who are also busy taking their own positions against us. We must get past the positions and focus on the common good.

As a process, mediation demands that the parties stop shouting at each other and begin to really communicate. To do this, they must first listen to each other. As part of the process, a mediator sets up a set of parameters, within which each party is given an opportunity to tell his or her perspective on the issues and the problems, without interruption by the other. Thereafter, the mediator may ask some questions toward clarifying the issues and identifying points of agreement. Depending on the types and difficulties of the issues and the number of parties involved, the procedures used may vary, but the mediator must ensure that communications remain open and that all options are fully reviewed. At times the mediator can be an "agent of reality," helping a group to recognize the improbability or unreasonableness of its "position." The mediator has no authority to force any resolution or agreement—that right is always reserved for the participating parties, who retain the power to achieve their own result. If the mediation works, the result is an agreement (usually written) crafted by the parties themselves, and to which each assents.

Of particular importance is that before two parties who are at odds can reach an agreement, something must occur inside each of them. Each must listen to the other, not just as a party but as a person. Unless each changes—unless one person begins to hear the other and to recognize the value of the "opponent" and his or her interests, together they will not achieve a favorable result. The change that must occur is spiritual and involves acceptance of the other. It requires as well that they forgive each other. It is in this process that they are changed, and become more like Christ.

This chapter does not attempt to identify precisely how to implement mediation at each level within the church wherever it is needed. Nor does it attempt to identify those individuals or groups who can best serve as mediators. What it does is to suggest the need for the availability of mediation as a process, to allow the diverse forces in the church at all levels to begin to lessen their degrees of separation, and to understand better the concerns and interests of one another. It suggests the need for those in the church who are not at peace with their colleagues, for whatever reason, to recognize mediation as a possible mechanism for improving their relationships and for resolving their differences—in the manner of true peacemakers.

We in the church do not benefit from internal conflicts and do not need to resort to taking each other to civil or ecclesiastical court. Those who love each other do not wage war and do not sue each other. Christians love each other. However, we don't always show it. Right now, in many arenas, we aren't showing it very well. We may disagree on the details and on the precise mechanics of the implementation, but fundamentally we are Christians—we identify with the label of those who love: "See how they love one another."

If our divisions are a serious threat to the spiritual growth of church members, then it is time for the various parties who are at odds to recognize the seriousness of their disagreements, to acknowledge the divisive effects of their conflicts, and to agree to resolve the differences. What unites us, of course, is the church itself and our common life in the Spirit. What separates (or threatens to separate) us is our disagreement on how best to live out our common belief in the Gospel, how to implement the commandment that Christ left us ("Love one another as I have loved you").

St. Francis de Sales (1567–1622) enjoined us to "Live Jesus!" Unfortunately we are in dispute as to how best we ought to do that! What unites us is far more important and fundamental than what threatens to separate us. We cannot afford not to make the effort to avoid dissension and contentiousness, and to mediate the disagreements that arise, as together we try to "Live Jesus."

QUESTIONS FOR REFLECTION AND DISCUSSION

1. How have the divisions in the church affected your spiritual and moral life?

2. Have you ever experienced mediation of a dispute? What was the outcome? Would you recommend mediation?

3. Can you think of other ways in which disputes in the church could be reconciled?

VIII. Growing Spiritually in Daily Life

$\mathcal{M}$oral and spiritual maturity is difficult to attain. All of the previous chapters, each in its own way, speak of the necessity of ongoing formation. Our consciences could be more completely conformed to the truth; our discernments could be more sensitive; our understanding of scripture could be more profound. In this life we will always have a long way to go.

This attitude stands in contrast to one prominent strand in American life. We live in the era of "superstars."[1] They are the focus of television, radio, magazines and newspapers. No popular movie or football team can be without a few such stars. These are the people that many American seek to imitate.

Maybe we ourselves would like to be such stars. We would love to see ourselves on television or have our pictures on the covers of newsmagazines. After all, we might think, even the church has its superstars. Pope John Paul II and Mother Teresa draw crowds and make the evening news. Their books sell millions. A bit of celebrity might not be a bad thing in this media age.

Such flights of fancy yield in time to the truth. A little reflection on the difference between celebrity and reality, between superstardom and substance, and between "hype" and fact, brings us to the much neglected virtue of humility. For humility is realism. And humility is what we need to become mature.

The humble person sees the world and the self with a clear eye. No wild imagination conceals the truth of things. No camera lens or inflated ego distorts the image. The humble person has his or her feet firmly on the ground.

Humility is realism. Humble people see their gifts or talents for what they are; they see their own human flaws and deficiencies as well. They neither deny their abilities nor overestimate them. They neither exalt nor debase themselves.

The humble people I know are unassuming. They are not continually trumpeting their accomplishments. While they will acknowledge their gifts if pressed, they tend rather to ask you about your daily life and concerns. They encourage you in your dreams and projects. The humble people I know tend to be good listeners. They see the value in each person and respect his or her goodness.

Humility is synonymous with thoughtfulness. Humble people will ask about your sick relative or friend. They are not superficial, but substantive. They can handle the media limelight but can also leave it to others. They have few illusions about the world and about human weakness.

There is more than a little courage in humility. It takes courage to look at our lives realistically. It takes courage to change our patterns of living. It takes courage to be a person of character when image, spin and proper positioning are valued.

Humility leads quickly to generosity. The humble people I know are quick to share. They give whatever they have. Their time, talent, money and energy are available to help others. One successful businessman I know has made it a goal to give away a million dollars in his lifetime. He urges others to do the same. He believes that God's blessings should be shared.

In humility, we live from the inside out. We operate from inner convictions about the good and the right. We know that we can always improve in our understanding of what is right and in our actions to achieve the good.

The path to humility sometimes comes through personal disillusionment, failure, grief or sickness. The death of a parent or spouse can be an occasion for the deep reflection characteristic of humility. The experiences of life teach us. We often learn the hard way. These experiences puncture our illusions of superiority or control. They show us that our strength is insufficient. They cut our proud egos down to size. They show us our need for the help of the Holy Spirit.

Paradoxically, humble people can also laugh. Having suffered, they can also enjoy. They can appreciate the good, the incongruous and the just plain crazy aspects of life. The humble person can take serious things seriously and the not-so-serious with good grace and humor.

In our humble realism, we realize that we are completely dependent on God. All our talents come from God. Without the grace of the Holy Spirit, we would be nothing. Through this grace we are everything.

The humble person knows that Jesus is the model. He "humbled himself accepting even death, death on a cross" (Phil 2:8). And he now sits at the right hand of the Father. He urged us to take the last place at banquets and to welcome sinners.

Celebrities seem to be preoccupied with their own feelings, thoughts and accomplishments. They love the best seats at televised banquets. The true superstars are not so self-centered. Spiritually mature people point beyond themselves to Christ. Christ is the real superstar.

Meeting Christ

We may encounter Jesus in a variety of ways in our daily lives. This may be in the beauty of the sunrise, in a Scripture verse read just after dawn, in the celebration of the eucharist in a neighboring church or in the generous action of a colleague at work.

Occasionally we may meet Christ in a special moment, one so striking that it stays with us for days or weeks. Some authors refer to these as "mystical moments." These are not the same as the mysticism of the great saints such as Teresa of Avila. But they are brief glimpses of the divine in the ordinary, deeper insights into Christ's revelation to us, or "the sudden awareness of an immediate and total presence of the overwhelming and awesome Divine Mystery to ourselves."[2]

The critical point here is that we can meet Christ in our daily lives. The humble person points to Christ through his or her deeds and life. Such a person never ceases to listen and look for Christ in her or his daily life. The humble person realizes that the search for spiritual maturity is a continual process.

Our moral growth is a daily phenomenon. It is in the ordinary events of life that we can meet God. We form our consciences and our characters in the decisions of daily life. Everyday life is the setting for our virtuous living.

QUESTIONS FOR REFLECTION AND DISCUSSION

1. Have you known people who have a humble realism about life? Has this helped them to become spiritually mature?

2. How have you experienced Christ's presence in your daily life?

Notes

I. LIVING IN THE SPIRIT

1. We will discuss discernment in detail in chapter 5.

2. See my *Friendship: Key to Spiritual Growth* (Mahwah, NJ: Paulist Press, 1997) for a more detailed discussion of the role of our relationships in spiritual growth.

3. Joseph Cardinal Bernardin, *The Gift of Peace* (Chicago: Loyola Press, 1997), pp. 5–6.

4. For more references to the Holy Spirit in Scripture, see my "The Holy Spirit: Personal and Salesian Reflections," *Review for Religious* (July-August 1983): 546.

5. St. Francis de Sales, *Treatise on the Love of God,* vol. II, trans. John K. Ryan (Rockford, IL: TAN Books, 1974), p. 211.

6. Catherine Walsh, "Perspectives," *America,* September 14, 1996, p. 8.

7. Some material in this chapter originally appeared in my article on the Holy Spirit, entitled "What is the Spirit Up To?" that appeared in *Faith Alive,* National Catholic News Service, 1997.

II. STUDYING AND PRAYING THE SCRIPTURES

1. See Thomas F. Dailey, O.S.F.S., "In Praise of God's Word: Biblical Studies since Vatican II," in *The Church in the '90s: Its Legacy, Its Future* (Collegeville, MN: Liturgical Press, 1993), pp. 50–62.

2. *Vatican Council II: The Conciliar and Post-Conciliar Documents,* ed. Austin Flannery, O.P. (Northport, NY: Costello Publishing Company, 1975), pp. 756–765.

3. See, for example, *The Collegeville Bible Commentaries* (Collegeville, MN: The Liturgical Press); Joseph A. Fitzmyer, S.J., in his *Scripture the Soul of Theology* (Mahwah, NJ: Paulist Press, 1994) elaborates many of the points made in this chapter in much greater depth.

III. PERSONAL GROWTH IN COMMUNITY

1. This theme is also central to Pope John Paul II's recent encyclical, *Evangelium Vitae,* which, in its very first sentence, asserts that "The Gospel of life is at the heart of Jesus' message," and goes on to assert the "sacred value of human life from its very beginning until its end." *Origins,* vol. 24 (April 6, 1995), pp. 689–730, paragraphs 1 and 2.

2. James S. Langelaan, "Man, the Image and Likeness of God," *Downside Review* 95 (1977): 40.

3. See Michael K. Duffey, *Be Blessed in What You Do* (Mahwah, NJ: Paulist Press, 1988), pp. 117–21.

4. John J. Conley, "Family, Tradition, Papacy," *America,* April 29, 1995, p. 20.

5. Council on Families in America, *Marriage in America: A Report to the Nation* (March, 1995), p. 4.

6. William Raspberry, "...At the Root of the Problem: Fatherlessness," *Washington Post,* March 22, 1995, p. A21. See also David Blankenhorn, *Fatherless America: Confronting Our Most Urgent Social Problem* (New York: Basic Books, 1995).

7. See Robert J. Samuelson, "Why Men Need Family Values," *Newsweek,* April 8, 1996, p. 43.

8. Robert N. Bellah, "Changing Values: A Challenge for Pastoral Planning and Practice," *National Conference of Catholic Bishops,* November 13, 1994, p. 8.

9. I wish to thank Mrs. Elizabeth Le Buffe for sharing this experience.

10. Catherine Walsh, "Perspectives," *America,* p. 5, February 11, 1995.

11. Robert Wuthnow, *Sharing the Journey: Support Groups and America's New Quest for Community* (New York: Free Press, 1994), p. 3.

12. Ibid., pp. 6, 7.

13. Alice S. Baum and Donald W. Burnes, "Rights and Responsibilities: A New Social Compact": draft article for *Spirit.*

14. Ibid., p. 3.

15. Robert Bellah et al., "The Good Society," adapted in *Commonweal,* July 12, 1991, p. 427.

16. Senator Bill Bradley, "America's Challenge: Revitalizing Our National Community," speech given at The National Press Club, Washington, D.C., February 9, 1995, p. 2.

17. Alice S. Baum and Donald W. Burnes, *A Nation in Denial: The Truth about Homelessness* (Boulder: Westview Press, 1993), p. 3.

IV. BELIEVING IN THE CHURCH TODAY

1. Robert Carlston, in a private communication to the author, February 9, 1993.

2. Craig Dykstra, "Shared Convictions," *Initiatives in Religion* 3 (Fall 1994): 3.

3. Peter Steinfels, "Now Is the Time: A Keynote Presentation," Leadership Conference of Women Religious/Conference of Major Superiors of Men, August 27, 1992, p. 12.

4. H. Richard McCord, "New Research Looks at Preparing Laity for Ministry," *Gifts,* 1994, #3, p. 1.

5. See Philip Murnion, *New Parish Ministers* (New York: National Pastoral Life Center, 1992).

6. See Sheila Garcia and John W. Crossin, O.S.F.S., "Collaboration: Joining Gifts and Talents," *Liguorian* 85 (June 1997): 48–53.

7. Margaret O'Brien Steinfels, "The Unholy Alliance between the Right and the Left in the Catholic Church," *America,* May 2, 1992, p. 376.

8. See Margaret O'Brien Steinfels, Letter to the Editor, *America,* October 10, 1992, p. 261.

9. See John Farrelly, O.S.B., *Belief in God in Our Time* (Collegeville, MN: The Liturgical Press, 1992).

10. Margaret O'Brien Steinfels, Address for De Sales School of Theology, October 22, 1992, p. 3.

11. John Jay Hughes, Letter to the Editor, *America,* September 19, 1992, p. 173.

12. *Optatam Totius* (Declaration on the Training of Priests, translation from *Vatican Council II: The Conciliar and Post-Conciliar Documents,* ed. Austin Flannery, O.P. [Northport, NY: Costello

Publishing Co., 1975]), October 28, 1965, paragraph 16, pp. 707–724.

13. See, for example, William E. May, *An Introduction to Moral Theology*, revised edition (Huntington, IN: Our Sunday Visitor, 1994) and Richard Gula, S.S., *Reason Informed by Faith: Foundations of Catholic Morality* (Mahwah, NJ: Paulist Press, 1989) for two contrasting approaches.

14. Pope John Paul II, *Veritatis Splendor, Origins*, October 14, 1993.

15. Mark O'Keefe, "Christian Prayer and Moral Decision Making," *Spiritual Life* 40 (Fall 1994): 140. See also Michael K. Duffey, *Be Blessed in What You Do: The Unity of Christian Ethics and Spirituality* (Mahwah, NJ: Paulist Press, 1988) and Mark O'Keefe, O.S.B., *Becoming Good, Becoming Holy* (Mahwah, NJ: Paulist Press, 1995).

16. See John W. Crossin, O.S.F.S., *Friendship: The Key to Spiritual Growth* (Mahwah, NJ: Paulist Press, 1997) for a more extensive discussion of this topic.

17. O'Keefe, *Becoming Good, Becoming Holy*, p. 177.

18. See Duffey, p. 126.

V. THE DYNAMIC CHRISTIAN CONSCIENCE

1. Jonathan Alter and Pat Wingert, "The Return of Shame," *Newsweek*, February 6, 1995, pp. 21–25.

2. John Glaser, "Conscience and Superego: A Key Distinction," *Theological Studies* 32 (1971): 30–47.

3. See William E. May, "Growing into the Human Conscientiously," in *Becoming Human: An Invitation to Christian Ethics* (Dayton, OH: Pflaum Publishing, 1975), pp. 53–77.

4. *Documents of Vatican II,* edited by Walter Abbott, S.J. (New York: Guild Press, 1965), "Pastoral Constitution on the Church in the Modern World," par. 16, p. 213.

5. See John Macquarrie, "Conscience, Sin, and Grace," in *Three Issues in Ethics* (New York: Harper and Row, 1970): 111–130.

6. Ibid., p. 112.

7. "Pastoral Constitution on the Church in the Modern World," paragraph 16.

8. Kevin D. O'Rourke and Philip Boyle, "Formation of Conscience," in *Medical Ethics: Sources of Catholic Teaching* (St. Louis: The Catholic Health Association, 1989), pp. 14–26.

9. See, Montague Brown, *The Quest for Moral Foundations: An Introduction to Ethics* (Washington, D.C.: Georgetown University Press, 1996) for a good exposition of natural law and its advantages over other moral systems.

10. See, for example, William E. May, "The Natural Law and Moral Life," in his *An Introduction to Moral Theology,* revised edition (Huntington, IN: Our Sunday Visitor, 1994), pp. 43–105 or Benedict M. Ashley and Kevin D. O'Rourke, *Healthcare Ethics,* fourth edition (Washington, D.C.: Georgetown University Press, 1997), pp. 139–176.

11. Canadian Catholic Conference, "The Formation of Conscience," *Catholic Mind,* April 1974, p. 42.

12. Macquarrie, p. 119.

13. Paul Philibert, "The Motors of Morality: Religion and Relation," in *Moral Development Foundations: Judeo-Christian Alternatives to Piaget/Kohlberg,* ed. Donald M. Joy (Nashville: Abingdon, 1983), pp. 87–110.

14. See my *What Are They Saying About Virtue?* (Mahwah, NJ:

Paulist Press, 1985), pp. 82–91 for a more detailed discussion of the pros and cons of Kohlberg's theory.

15. See Cynthia S. W. Crysdale, "Gilligan and the Ethics of Care: An Update," *Religious Studies Review* 20/1(January 1994): 21–28 for a review and analysis of Gilligan's work.

16. Christopher Lasch, "Gilligan's Island," *The New Republic,* December 7, 1992, p. 36.

17. Ibid., p. 38.

18. See Philibert, pp. 94–104 for the basis of what follows.

19. William E. May in his *An Introduction to Moral Theology* argues that "lack of assent" is the proper way to speak and think of the issue commonly referred to as "dissent."

20. Macquarrie, p. 117.

21. Sidney Callahan, "Conscience Reconsidered," *America,* November 1, 1986, p. 252.

22. David Bohr, *Catholic Moral Tradition* (Huntington, IN: Our Sunday Visitor, 1990), p. 172.

VI. MORAL DISCERNMENT

1. See Benedict Ashley and Kevin O'Rourke, *Healthcare Ethics: A Theological Analysis,* fourth edition (Washington, D.C.: Georgetown University Press, 1997), pp. 139–223.

2. John Paul II, *Evangelium Vitae, Origins,* April 6, 1995, pp. 689–730.

3. John H. Wright, S.J., "Discernment of Spirits in the New Testament," in *Spiritual Direction: Contemporary Readings,* ed. with introductions by Kevin Culligan, O.C.D. (Locust Valley, NY: Living Flame Press, 1983), pp. 168–79.

4. See Richard J. Sweeney, "Discernment in the Spiritual Direction of St. Francis de Sales," *Review for Religious* 39 (1980): 127–41. Much of the discussion which follows draws on his work. Also see my "Discernment: The Spirituality of St. Francis de Sales and Contemporary Perspectives," in *Salesian Spirituality: Catalyst to Collaboration*, ed. William J. Ruhl, O.S.F.S. (Washington, D.C.: De Sales School of Theology, 1993), pp. 95–110.

5. Sweeney, p. 135.

6. See my article, "Obedience," in *The New Dictionary of Theology*, eds. Joseph A Komonchak, Mary Collins and Dermot A. Lane (Wilmington: Michael Glazier, 1987), pp. 720–21.

7. Washington: United States Catholic Conference, 1994.

8. *Lumen Gentium* (The Dogmatic Constitution on the Church), November 21, 1964, sections 18–28, translation in *Vatican Council II: The Conciliar and Post-Conciliar Documents*, pp. 369–387.

9. See Avery Dulles, S. J., *The Resilient Church* (Garden City, NY: Doubleday, 1977), chapter 5 for more on authority in the church.

VII. WORKING IN FAITH SO THAT ALL MAY BE ONE

1. The initial statement for the project was prepared by the National Pastoral Life Center (18 Bleecker Street, New York, NY 10012) and is entitled "Called to Be Catholic: Church in a Time of Peril." Some of the articles addressing this project are: Kenneth E. Untener, "How Bishops Talk," *America*, October 19, 1996, pp. 9–15; Robert Imbelli, "'Common Ground' as Communion—A Witness for the Defense," *National Catholic Register*, December 22–28, 1996, p. 7; Ladislas Orsy, "'A Wonderful Exchange,'" *America*, January 4, 1997, p. 3; Avery Dulles, "Travails of Dialogue," *Crisis*, February, 1997, pp. 16–21; Deal W. Hudson, "No Quick Fixes," *Crisis*, April, 1997, p. 4; and Joseph Komonchak,

"On the People of God as a Theological and Sociological Reality: The Case for Dialogue," *National Catholic Register,* June 8–14, 1997, p. 5.

2. See my *Friendship: The Key to Spiritual Growth* (Mahwah, NJ: Paulist Press, 1997), where personal reconciliation and healing is considered in chapter 7.

3. Stephen J. Rosetti, "Parishes as Victims of Abuse," *Human Development* 14/4 (Winter, 1993): 19.

4. See "How to Handle Criticism," *New Life Center,* Fall, 1994, p. 4.

5. Loughlan Sofield, S.T., and Carroll Juliano, S.H.C.J., *Collaborative Ministry* (Notre Dame, IN: Ave Maria Press, 1987), pp. 102, 104.

6. Ibid., p. 104.

7. Ibid., p. 108.

8. Ibid., p. 110.

VIII. GROWING SPIRITUALLY IN DAILY LIFE

1. The following section, originally entitled "Humility: Is There Any Hope for It?" first appeared in the *Faith Alive* series of the Catholic News Service, 1995.

2. Matthias Neuman, "Mystical Moments in Daily Life," *Review for Religious* 56 (January-February 1997): 78.

Annotated Bibliography

Bohr, David. *Catholic Moral Tradition.* Huntington, IN: Our Sunday Visitor Publishing Division, 1990.
> *Bohr's text gives a more detailed development of many of the moral topics—such as conscience and discernment—discussed in this book.*

Brown, Montague. *The Quest for Moral Foundations: An Introduction to Ethics.* Washington: Georgetown University Press, 1996.
> *This clearly written and nontechnical book offers a concise discussion of contemporary ethical systems. It advances a natural law philosophy as the most sensible approach to the quest for moral foundations.*

Collegeville Bible Commentaries. Collegeville, MN: The Liturgical Press.
> *This series of affordable paperbacks gives a well-written introduction to the biblical books. The commentary is below the text and is not so extensive as to be tedious or boring to the educated nonspecialist. There are questions for discussion or personal reflection at the end of the booklet.*

O'Keefe, Mark. *Becoming Good, Becoming Holy: On the Relationship of Christian Ethics and Spirituality.* Mahwah, NJ: Paulist Press, 1995.
> *In this series of related essays, O'Keefe explores this heretofore neglected topic—the relationship of ethics and spirituality—in ways that will expand many of the themes discussed in this book.*

Sofield, Loughlan, S.T., and Carroll Juliano, S.H.C.J. *Collaborative Ministry: Skills and Guidelines.* Notre Dame, IN: Ave Maria Press, 1987.
The authors offer a solid introduction to a topic that is becoming increasingly important in the contemporary church.

Index